Houses and Society in the
Later Roman Empire

BRISTOL CLASSICAL PRESS DEBATES IN ARCHAEOLOGY
Series editor: Richard Hodges

Against Cultural Property John Carman
Archaeology: The Conceptual Challenge Timothy Insoll
Archaeology and Text John Moreland
Archaeology and the Pan-European Romanesque Tadhg O'Keeffe
Beyond Celts, Germans and Scythians Peter S. Wells
Combat Archaeology John Schofield
Debating the Archaeological Heritage Robin Skeates
Early Islamic Syria Alan Walmsley
Gerasa and the Decapolis David Kennedy
Houses and Society in the Later Roman Empire Kim Bowes
Image and Response in Early Europe Peter S. Wells
Indo-Roman Trade Roberta Tomber
Loot, Legitimacy and Ownership Colin Renfrew
Lost Civilization: The Contested Islamic Past in Spain and Portugal James L. Boone
Museums and the Construction of Disciplines Christopher Whitehead
The Origins of the English Catherine Hills
Rethinking Wetland Archaeology Robert Van de Noort & Aidan O'Sullivan
The Roman Countryside Stephen Dyson
Shipwreck Archaeology of the Holy Land Sean Kingsley
Social Evolution Mark Pluciennik
State Formation in Early China Li Liu & Xingcan Chen
Towns and Trade in the Age of Charlemagne Richard Hodges
Villa to Village Riccardo Francovich & Richard Hodges

Houses and Society in the Later Roman Empire

Kim Bowes

Bristol Classical Press

Published by Bristol Classical Press 2012

Bristol Classical Press, an imprint of Bloomsbury Publishing Plc

Bloomsbury Publishing Plc
50 Bedford Square
London WC1B 3DP
www.bloomsburyacademic.com

Copyright © Kim Bowes 2010

First published by Gerald Duckworth & Co. Ltd. 2010

The author has asserted her rights under the Copyright, Designs and Patents Act 1988 to be identified as the author of this work.

ISBN: 978 0 7156 3882 8

A CIP catalogue record for this book is available from the British Library

Typeset by Ray Davies

Caution

All rights reserved. No part of this publication may be reproduced in any form or by any means – graphic, electronic or mechanical, including information storage and retrieval systems – without the prior written permission of Bloomsbury Publishing Plc.

This book is produced using paper that is made from wood grown in managed, sustainable forests. It is natural, renewable and recyclable. The logging and manufacturing processes conform to the environmental regulations of the country of origin.

Contents

List of Illustrations 9
Introduction 11

1. Inventing the Later Roman House 19
2. The Archaeology of Later Roman Houses 35
3. Houses and History 61
4. New Directions 85

Bibliography 101
Index 117

For LOML

List of Illustrations

Fig. 1. Palace of the Dux, Apollonia, Libya, plan (Goodchild 1976, fig. 1).   12
Fig. 2. Villa di Casale, Piazza Armerina, Sicily, plan (Gentili 1999, fig. 14).   12
Fig. 3. Villa di Casale, Piazza Armerina, Sicily: mosaic of the Great Hunt, detail (author).   13
Fig. 4. Triconch Palace, Butrint, Albania, phased plans (Gilkes and Lako 2004, figs 9.4, 9.8, 9.12).   14
Fig. 5. Villa at Carranque, Spain, fourth century, plan (Chavarría 2007, 86).   15
Fig. 6. Palace of Diocletian, Split, Croatia, plan (Baldini Lippolis 2001, fig. 2).   21
Fig. 7. Comparison of Piazza Armerina, plan, with reconstruction of church of S. Paulo fuori le Mura, as reproduced by H.P. L'Orange, *Art Forms and Civic Life* (1965, figs 26-7).   24
Fig. 8. House of the Hunt (and to north, House of the New Hunt), Bulla Regia, Tunisia, plan (Baldini Lippolis 2001, p. 166).   27
Fig. 9. House of the Valerii, Rome, plan (after Brenk 1999, fig. 3).   30
Fig. 10. House plans from Athens: House of Proclus, House between Dyonisiou Areopagitou and Makri Streets, and House between Irodou Attikou 2 and Basilissis Sofias Streets (Baldini Lippolis 2001, pp. 151-2).   36-7

Houses and Society in the Later Roman Empire

Fig. 11. Hanghaus 1, Ephesus, Turkey, plan of late fourth-century phase (Lang-Auinger 1996, pl. 6). — 40

Fig. 12. Hanghaus 2.4, Ephesus, Turkey, mid-third-century phase plans with find assemblages (after Thür 2002, fig. 25 and Thür 2005). — 42-3

Fig. 13. Bishop's House, Aphrodisias, plan (Berenfeld 2002). — 45

Fig. 14. Theatre House, Ephesus, Turkey, plan showing Hellenistic and late antique phases (Thür 2002b, fig. 7). — 47

Fig. 15. Hanghaus 2.6, Ephesus, plan of third-century phase (Thür 2002a, taf. 44). — 48

Fig. 16. Maison à l'Ouest du Palais du Gouverneur and Maison aux demi-Colonnes, Volubilis, Morocco, plans (after Etienne 1960, pl. VIII, XIV). — 50-1

Fig. 17. Maison d'Europe and Maison de Bacchus, Djemila, Tunisia, plans (Blanchard-Lemée 1975, fig. 49; Baldini Lippolis 2001, p. 195). — 53

Fig. 18. Reconstruction of a segmented wooden *stibadium* from the Villa of the Falconer, Argos (Åkerstrom Hougen 1974, fig. 74). — 56

Fig. 19. Villas of Cuevas de Soria and Gárgoles, Spain, plans (Chavarría 2007, figs 65, 85). — 59

Fig. 20. Ephesus, city plan showing late antique houses and late antique urban improvements (after Foss 1979, fig. 12). — 75

Fig. 21. Map of the Roman empire showing concentrations of monumentalized rural villas. — 92

Fig. 22. Some villas of the Midi-Pyrénées/Aquitaine, France: Montmaurin, Lescar and Jurançon, plans (Balmelle 2001, figs 294, 280, 273). — 96-7

Fig. 23. Houses of Djemila, Tunisia: Maison de l'Ane and Maison aux Stucs, plans (Blanchard-Lemée 1975, figs 49, 82). — 98-9

Introduction

Houses, we like to assume, are mirrors; they reflect the social environment in which they were created. It is these reflective qualities that make houses historically interesting; burnish the mirror bright enough through careful excavation and spatial analysis, and houses can be made to reflect back the society that produced them (Rapoport 1969; Bourdieu 1977; Blanton 1994). The monotonous sameness of the houses from Greek cities reflects their egalitarian democracies (Hoepfner and Schwander 1986); the fortified houses of medieval French lords echo the rise of a military aristocracy (Duby, Barthélemy, Roncière 1988), while a warren of specialized rooms characterizes the Victorian predilection for ordered behaviour (Cromley 2003, 165-71). On this same principle, the house should be an important barometer of social change; just as the appearance of posh mansions heralded the rise of Hellenistic monarchies, or a preoccupation with kitchen gadgets charts the rise of Post-War consumerism (Hellman 2004), so, too, the progress from the late republic to late antiquity should be marked in the stones of the empire's houses.

The elite homes of the third to sixth centuries AD do not disappoint. In their architecture and decoration, they form one of the largest bodies of material culture from the late empire. Close to a thousand such houses have been excavated in both city and countryside – urban townhouses like the austere Palace of the Dux in Apollonia (Susa, Libya) (Fig. 1), and sprawling rural villas, like the mosaic-covered Piazza Armerina (central Sicily) (Figs 2-3). Excavation reveals new examples each year, from the splendid, unfinished Triconch Palace in

Houses and Society in the Later Roman Empire

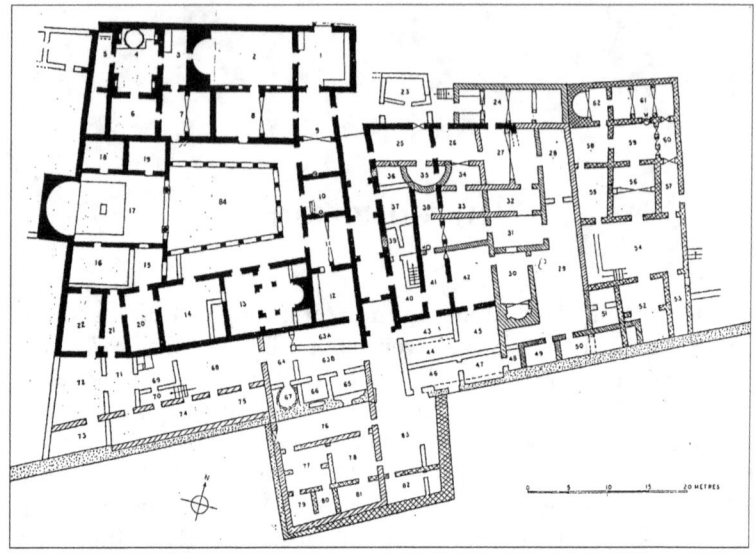

Fig. 1. Palace of the Dux, Apollonia, Libya.

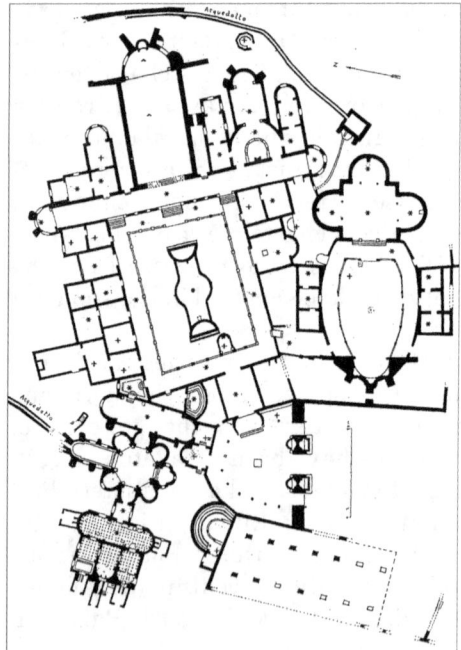

Fig. 2. Villa di Casale, Piazza Armerina, Sicily.

Introduction

Fig. 3. Villa di Casale, Piazza Armerina, Sicily: Mosaic of the Great Hunt (detail).

Butrint on the shores of modern Albania (Fig. 4), to the jewel-like villa of Carranque outside Madrid with its fanciful mosaics and adjacent great mausoleum (Fig. 5).

As with the houses of ancient Greece or medieval France, the walls and floors of these houses have naturally been rummaged for clues to the particular character of late antique

Houses and Society in the Later Roman Empire

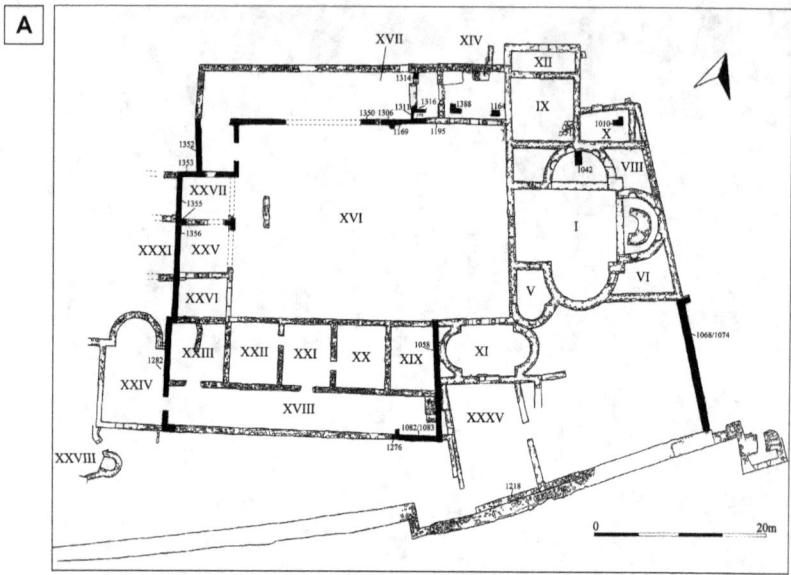

Fig. 4. Triconch Palace, Butrint, Albania. A: Phase 1 (third century and earlier); B: Phase 2 (fourth century); C (*opposite above*): Phase 3 (early fifth century).

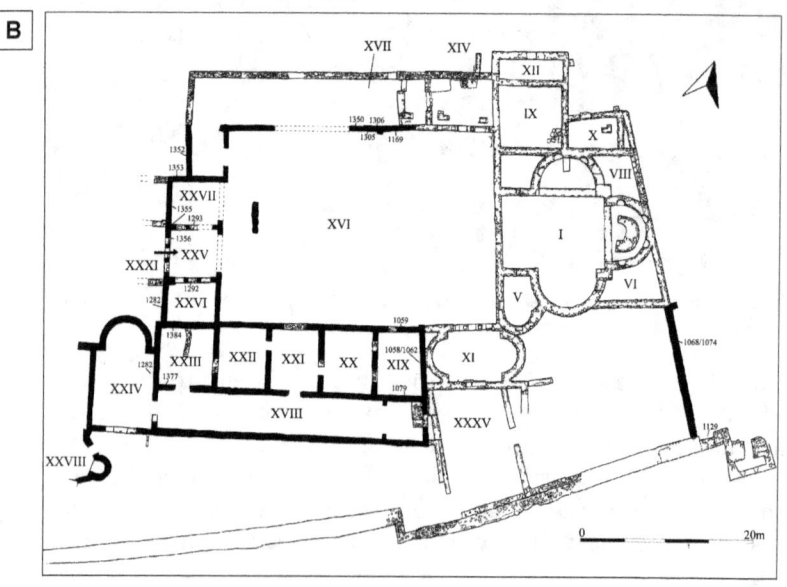

Introduction

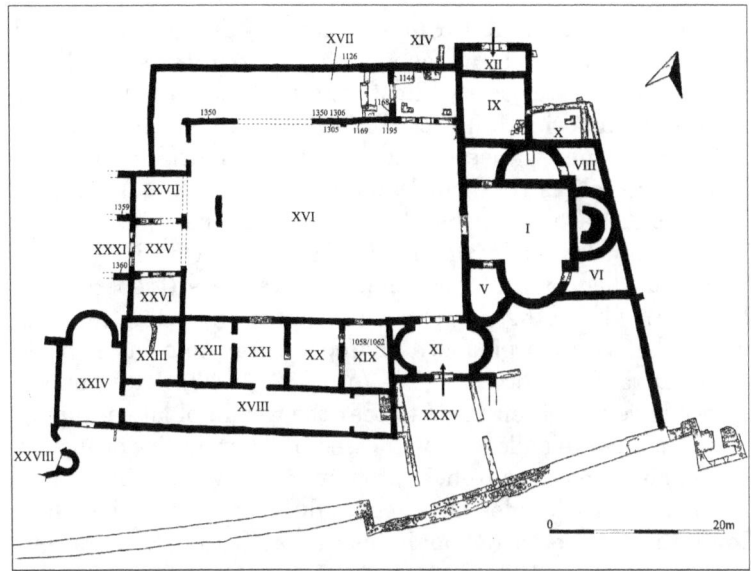
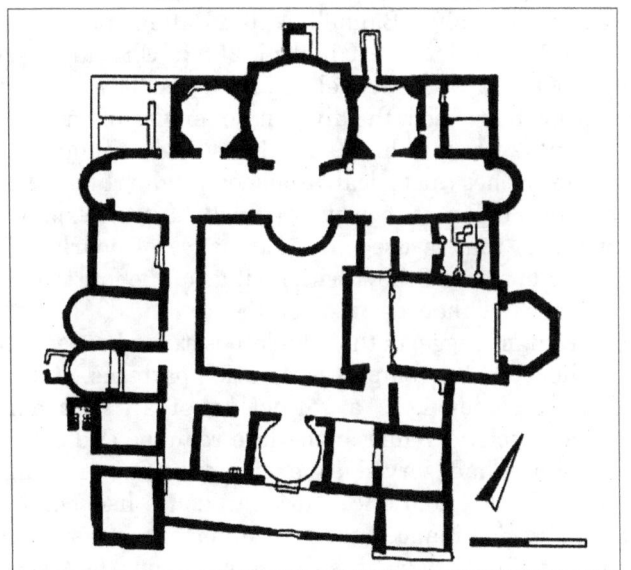

Fig. 5. Villa at Carranque, Spain, fourth century.

society. For the great turn-of-the-century historian Michael Rostovzteff, the great villas of the late empire spelled the creation of a 'caste society' (Rostovzteff 1926, 474 n. 6); for the Italian art historian Ranuccio Bianchi Bandinelli, the mosaics of African homes witnessed the rise of a provincial proletariat over Italian elites (Bianchi Bandinelli 1971, 223-61). Studies preoccupied with collapse of the ancient city have blamed the great urban *domus* for the death of participatory city government, quashed by a narrow clique of grandees (Liebeschuetz 2001, 37), while others have read from the sprawling remains of rural villas a marginalized and oppressed proto-feudal peasantry (Carandini, Ricci and De Vos 1982, 15-23). Late antique houses have thus been made to bear the weight of late antiquity itself, a period that allegedly witnessed the slow decline of ancient social habits and the advent of proto-medieval ways of life.

The last two decades have seen a flurry of new work on late Roman houses, both regionally-based catalogues, and conceptual studies (Ellis 1988; Thébert 1987; Van Osssel 1992; Sodini 1995; 1997; Scott 2000; Balmelle 2001; Baldini Lippolis 2002; Mulvin 2002; Bullo and Ghedini 2003; Chavarría 2007; Sfameni 2006b; Lavan, Özgenel and Sarantis 2007). This scholarship naturally reflects the diversity of environments (urban, rural, East, West) in which such houses are found and the various approaches (historical, archaeological, art historical) of its raconteurs. It shares, however, a fairly uniform explanatory paradigm, one that is used to make sense of nearly all late Roman elite homes, be they British villas of the fourth century or Asia Minor townhouses of the sixth.

The paradigm suggests that the late antique house, with its apsed audience halls, complex circulation patterns, and splendid reception rooms, is a reflection of an increasingly hierarchized society. While in the late republic and early empire the house had served as a site of social exchange or competition, by the fourth century the house had become an instrument of dominance, used to manage harsher forms of patronage, enforce sharper social distinctions between unequals, and stage ritualized meetings between peers.

Introduction

This short book offers a critical re-examination of late Roman houses, particularly the house as social artifact. Following that historiography, it focuses on houses of pretension, whose architecture or decoration shows some indication of luxury. In urban contexts these houses are typically termed *domus*, while in rural areas they are labelled *villae* (see Strube 1973 on shifting ancient terminologies). The book will suggest that the paradigms used to make sense of these houses are based in part around medieval-oriented teleologies and have read onto the archaeology an *a priori*, highly periodized vision of late antique society. Advances in the quantity and quality of archaeological data and new directions in social history suggest that these paradigms are in need of revision. The claims for new forms of spatial patterning have been exaggerated even as continuity with earlier trends has been underemphasized. Similarly, new work is revealing rather different urban and rural contexts for these houses, suggesting a more continuous picture of patronage, urban maintenance and landholding. What is 'new' about these houses, the book concludes, is their particular architectural aesthetics, and their clustered chronologies and geographies. Late antique houses, it is argued, should be understood not as products of hierarchization, but as hotspots of social competition, brought about by the Diocletianic and Constantinian economic and social reforms and their aftermaths.

The parameters of this study are largely determined by the trajectories of previous scholarship. Thus, 'elite houses' are considered to be any urban *domus* or rural villa with luxury provisions, typically considered mosaic floors, sculpture, painting or other decoration, bath suites and/or reception spaces. This formally-based definition privileges the Mediterranean peristyle house and its traditional comfort apparatus. Left out are certain regional housing forms, such as the monumental *gsur* of the Libyan pre-desert (Barker [ed.] 1996, vol. 1, 349) or the fine village houses of the Syrian massif (Tchalenko 1953-9), which, as local forms of 'elite' housing, merit inclusion. Mention will be made of these houses in so far as their exclusion from most social-historical house studies reveals important biases, but a full treatment is reserved for a forthcoming longer study that considers them in their local context.

Apart from these exclusions, the qualifier 'elite' here is left purposefully broad and again following the scholarship, vaguely defined. That is, the houses of 'elites' will be considered those which have the physical signs of pretension. In this way, 'elite' is actually defined by the house itself, rather defining houses through their owners' putative social categories, such as senatorial or curatorial elites. This approach has the advantage of making material culture an agent in, rather than simply bystander to, acts of social distinction. It also produces a critical apparatus that begins with the material culture itself, rather from houses defined by their affiliation with particular social classes. Thus, the few known examples of imperial palaces are mentioned throughout, but not made an object of particularized study except where historiography mandates. Likewise, some houses identified as 'episcopal palaces' are included among the general mass of elite housing but are not singled out as a particular category: recent research emphasizing the shared qualities of imperial, episcopal and other kinds of elite houses supports this approach. (Duval 1978; Ceylan 2007, 185).

1
Inventing the Later Roman House

The study of classical Greek and earlier Roman housing has undergone important revisions in recent years. Early work on the late classical Greek *oikos* and on late republican/early imperial houses drew its principal interpretive apparatus from ancient textual descriptions. Xenophon and Vitruvius, respectively, were relied upon as guides to ancient architectural practice and domestic behaviour, and archaeological interpretation followed their lead. Greek houses were believed to be starkly divided into male and female quarters (so-called *andronitis* and *gynaikonitis*), while earlier Roman houses were thought to follow a rigorous schema of architectural proportions, defining rooms of particularized function and access (Keuls 1985, 210-12; Mau 1899). These texts likewise enforced the notion of a generalized house 'type', thought to be typified in one or two major archaeological sites (Olynthos and Pompeii respectively) and produced by largely homogeneous societies (Hoepfner and Schwandner 1986; Graham 1966). These house norms were thus seen as yardsticks or barometers of cultural belonging, departure from them representing incomplete 'Hellenization' or 'Romanization'.

More recent work has turned away from these seemingly descriptive texts and the paradigms they helped produce, drawing on spatial and artifactual analysis that foregrounds the houses themselves over their ancient interpreters (Ault and Nevett 1999; Allison 2001). Attention to the decorative schemes of Pompeian houses, for instance, suggested the inapplicability of modern notions of 'private' space to ancient houses (Wallace-Hadrill 1994). Space syntax analysis, which maps access and permeability of spaces within the home, has revealed the enormous diversity of spatial patterning in Roman houses across the wealth spectrum (Grahame 2000). Artifact analysis – studying small finds like pots, tools and jewellery from living levels within their particular spatial find-spots – has largely demolished the notion of a successfully gender-divided Greek *oikos*, and has revealed the extraordinarily multifunctionality of all ancient house spaces: dining rooms might be used for sleeping, courtyards for stabling animals, bedrooms for parties or storage (Nevett 1999; Allison 2004; 2006; Berry 1997). More work on houses outside the 'canonical' sites and greater attention to variation within these sites have disabused us of the notion of a homogeneous 'Greek' house or even a 'Pompeian' house, exposing the enormous variety of domestic lived experience and the complex relationship between cultural affiliation and domestic form (Cahill 2002; Hales 2003). Finally, the texts are now read not as domestic Baedekers, but as moral treatises and social commentaries in which the notional concept of 'house' is used to order and critique society (Riggsby 1997; Nevett 1999; Henderson 2004). Thus, in disavowing an easy relationship with contemporary texts, the study of Greek and earlier Roman houses is slowly complicating an easy relationship between houses and their concomitant 'societies', and emphasizing instead the dialectical relationship between individual inhabitants, the structures they build and/or modify, and broader social behaviours.

The study of the later Roman house has proceeded from a very different evidentiary basis, and for the most part, from very different goals and methodologies. There is no Pompeii or Olynthos for the late Roman world, no cache of well-preserved houses from a wide range of social classes. Just as the existence of Pompeii fundamentally impacted the use of Roman houses to write social history, so the absence of such a corpus for the later empire meant that the field developed from and long coalesced around the most visually-gripping and historically-recognizable houses – imperial palaces. For scholars of the

1. Inventing the Later Roman House

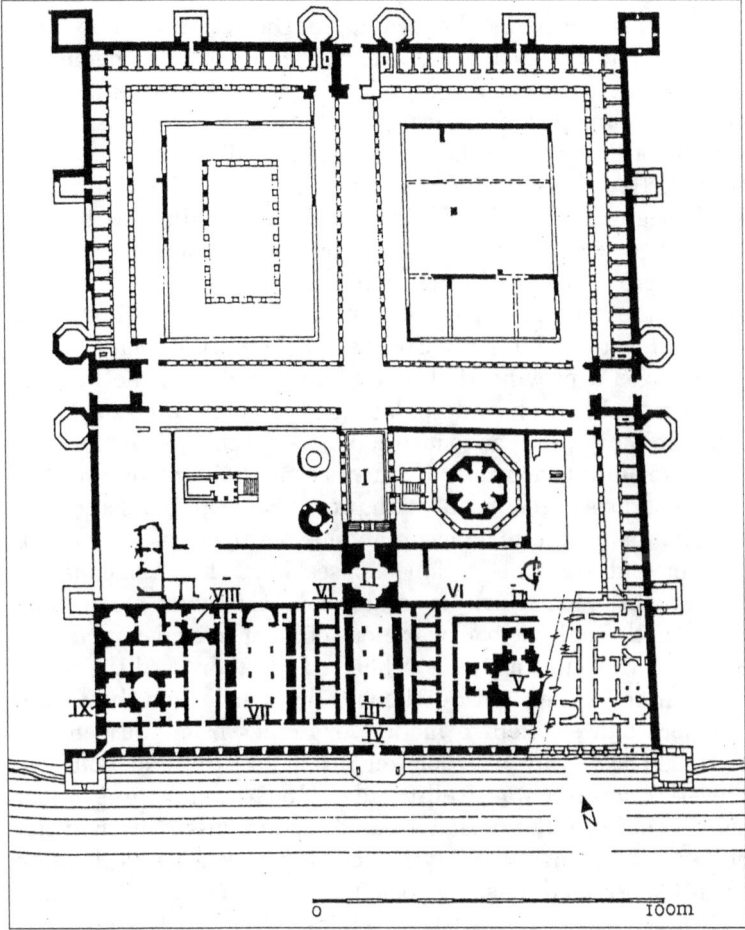

Fig. 6. Palace of Diocletian, Split, Croatia.

early twentieth century, the only known late antique residences were the so-called Palace of Diocletian at Split (Fig. 6) and the corpus of Syrian houses published by the Comte de Vogüé in 1865-77 (Adam 1764; Vogüe 1875-7). These examples were woven into formalistic histories aimed at elucidating the origins of medieval architecture, be it the Byzantine church or the monastic cloister. Beginning in Diocletian's palace and spreading to other houses, symmetrical room arrangements and the use of arcaded colonnades denoted the beginnings of medieval church and palace forms. The first two book-length studies of late antique houses were framed along these lines: Léon de Beylié postulated a new, eastern-derived architectural style, begun in Syria, evident at Split, disseminated through the largely unknown imperial palace at Constantinople and from there to Byzantine church architecture. Karl Swoboda located the origins of this new style in German villas of the imperial period, but saw Split as the palatial vector which popularized a provincial style and delivered it to the Romanesque church, cloister and palace (Beylié 1902; Swoboda 1919). While they disagreed as to its origins, these scholars all tended to view late antique domestic architecture as 'different' from that of earlier periods, already ripe with proto-medieval forms and thus a vector that connected ancient and medieval worlds. From their scholarly advent, late antique houses were thus embedded in medieval-oriented teleologies and their architecture persistently regarded through the backward lens of the medieval church.

Thus, when in the 1960s scholars first addressed the social implications of late antique houses (by which time the extant numbers had swollen to include examples from Antioch and North Africa), the path leading from late antique house to Christian church was well-trodden. Indeed, the three major house studies of the period all drew upon house-church evolution as their principal analytic tool. Enjar Dyggve's explication of an open-roofed 'basilica ipetrale/discoperta' in both palace and early Christian churches, Irving Lavin's hypothesis of evolution from palace *triclinium* or dining room to martyr's triconch, and H.P. L'Orange's emphasis on axial symmetry as a defining aspect of church and palace (see Fig. 7), all regarded late antique palaces through the backward gaze of a triumphant Christianity (Dyggve 1941; 1961; Lavin 1962; L'Orange 1965, 70-85, 76-9, 79-83). For Lavin and L'Orange, shared social behaviours might also be read backwards from these forms. Thus, the ceremonies of the imperial palace (derived

1. Inventing the Later Roman House

from textual sources) shared the same absolutist strictures as the ceremonies of the Christian liturgy, and the general architectural parallels – use of the apse, symmetrical and/or centralized plans, arcaded colonnades – were presumed to reflect a shared ritualized, sacral context – the 'palatium sacrum'. The late antique palace was thus an architectural manifestation of a rigid, autocratic society in which all movement was carefully orchestrated around the holiest of holies, the emperor himself.

The large-scale excavations of the mosaic-covered Villa di Casale at Piazza Armerina in central Sicily during the 1950s both helped to break the field's palace-bias, and, somewhat contradictorily, offered a broader field for the application of those same palace-based social ideologies (see Figs 2-3). Although its excavator identified the site as the palace of the emperor Maximian, others objected, claiming the villa was simply a particularly fine rural residence (Gentili 1951; Pace 1955; Dyggve 1956). In particular, Noël Duval penned a series of articles objecting to Piazza Armerina's palace identification on historical, topographic and architectural grounds, and more importantly, demolished the notion of a consistent, late antique 'palace architecture' (Duval 1961; 1978; 1997). While his arguments have been widely accepted and the field moved gradually away from a preoccupation with imperial palaces, the social-historical edifice built on the back of those palace identifications – the notion of a rigid, symmetrical architecture reflecting a rigid, ritualized society – remained intact.

Indeed, as a non-imperial residence which seemed imperial in its grandeur, Piazza Armerina seemed to offer material confirmation for the Dominate's 'trickle-down' effect on later Roman society – the notion that an increasingly autocratic government produced autocratic behaviours in elites. This idea was articulated most forcefully by historian Michael Rostovzteff (1926, 449-87, esp. 477). Under Rostovzteff's influence, Ranuccio Bianchi Bandinelli formulated the notion of an 'aulic' art in which the styles produced by an opulent court were parroted by autocratic elites; the mosaics of Piazza Armerina

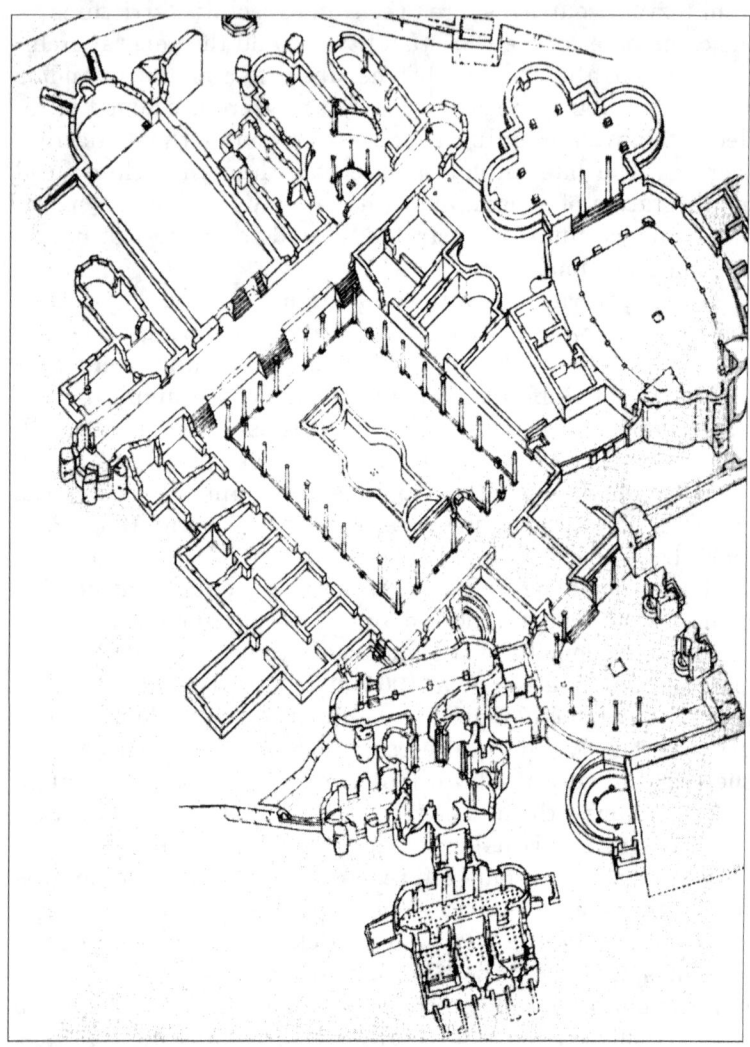

Fig. 7. Comparison of Piazza Armerina with the church of S. Paulo fuori le Mura (*opposite*), as it appeared in H.P. L'Orange, *Art Forms and Civic Life* (1965).

1. Inventing the Later Roman House

were a signal part of such a culture (Bianchi Bandinelli 1971, 33, 237-47). But it was Bandinelli's student, Andrea Carandini, whose two-volume monograph on Piazza Armerina, its decoration and rural context, found Rostovsteff's ideas applied most convincingly, not simply to the mosaics, but to the whole estate as a machine for rural exploitation (Carandini, Ricci and De Vos 1982, esp. 15-26). For Carandini, Piazza Armerina was the culmination of a social-historical narrative he had developed during his excavations of the late republican villa of Settefinestre. While Settefinestre marked the end of the republican farmer and the rise of the 'slave villa', Piazza Armerina witnessed the rise of the late antique tenant (Carandini, Ricci and De Vos 1982, 15-22; Carandini 1985; cf. Rostovzteff 1926, 465-6, 475-7). After the slave system imploded, rent farming to dependent tenants, the *coloni*, eventually took its place; the *coloni*, ground down by burdensome taxes and high rents, were displaced to nearby villages, at Piazza Armerina the putative estate *vicus* at nearby Sofiana (cf. Adamesteanu 1984). Richly decorated villas like Piazza Armerina were thus emblematic of a new hands-on approach to land management; previously absentee, elites now settled down in the countryside to keep an eye on their investment and built sumptuous residences to indulge their penchant for luxury living and mark their dominance over their inferiors. As suggested by Salvatore Settis' careful elucidation of Piazza Armerina's mosaics and by its many dining and reception halls, progress through such villas assumed the measured tread of an imperial march, as the autocratic position of senatorial elites on their estates mimicked the rituals of an autocratic court (Settis 1975; cf. Carandini, Ricci and De Vos 1982, 58-89). Piazza Armerina thus marked the penetration of palace social structures into the farthest corners of the house.

This residual tendency to view the sociology of the later Roman house through imperially-coloured glasses was broken by two major studies of the 1980s, by Yvon Thébert and Simon Ellis (Thèbert 1987; Ellis 1988). Their short articles offered the first explicitly socio-spatial analysis of later houses, pairing a detailed spatial discussion of select examples with particular models of late antique social history. Thébert's contribution to the popular *History of Private Life* series offered a nuanced introduction to the social life in North African urban houses, making a number of observations on their late antique phases (Thèbert 1987, 338-9, 379-80, 389-90; 2003, 482-3). Using a variety of examples and phased excavation data, Thébert was alert to the 'life-lines' of houses over their century-long occupation, and the social implications of shifting walls and entrances. He emphasized, although rarely elaborated on, the hierarchical nature of these later phases, drawing particularly on the House of the Hunt at Bulla Regia with its apsed hall with transept (Fig. 8). Echoing L'Orange's theories, Thébert claimed these halls focused the viewers' attention on a single point, the apse, thereby producing a hierarchical orientation. Private baths, he suggested, became more common over time, a signal of the elite's withdrawal from the crush of civic life and maintenance of more vertiginous social hierarchies. A compartmentalization of spaces into more discrete units through later dividing walls he similarly attributed to both hierarchization

1. Inventing the Later Roman House

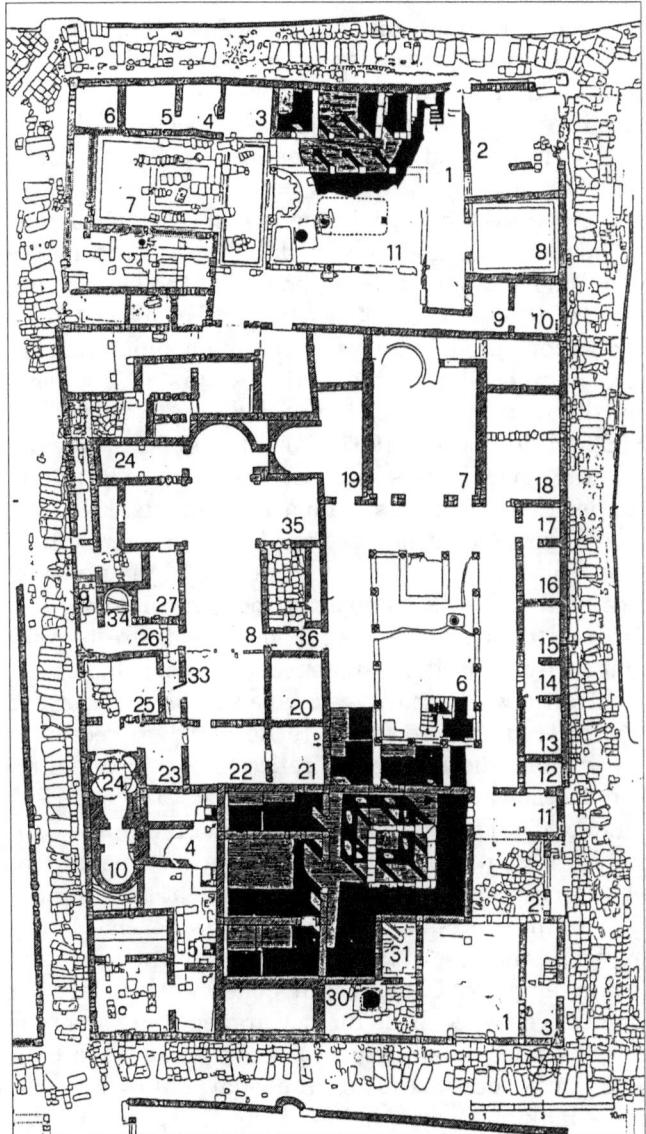

Fig. 8. House of the Hunt (and to north, House of the New Hunt), Bulla Regia, Tunisia.

and a concomitant emphasis on privacy and the individual. The harsh division between the landowning few and the propertyless masses that characterized Thébert's historical writings was thus revealed in the period's homes, which wore the inward-looking, stern face of an increasingly 'private' world (cf. Thèbert 1988, 323-4).

Ellis, arguably the most influential recent scholar on the later Roman house, drew his models largely, but not exclusively, around a group of urban houses of the eastern empire (Ellis 1985; 1988; 1991; 1997a; 1997b). He argued that the appearance of apsed dining and reception halls derived not only from imperial mimicry, but new tastes in furniture, namely the development of the *stibadium*, or curved dining couch (Ellis 1991, 119-20; 1997a). What was socially significant about late Roman houses was not their imperial origins, he argued, but their internal spatial arrangements: Ellis claimed that apsed rooms identified as reception halls were often spatially separated from those identified as dining rooms, for instance in the so-called Palace of the Dux in Apollonia (see Fig. 1). He attributed this distinction to a desire to separate different classes of visitors – the reception rooms built near the house entrance were meant to receive socially inferior clients, while interior dining rooms were designed to receive one's peers. For Ellis, these divisions reflected the broadening gulf between the *potentissimi* and their *clientes* and the rise of a more autocratic form of patronage (Ellis 1988, 574-5; 1991, 120-3, 130; 1997a). Even interactions between peers took on more hierarchical arrangements. The apse of the dining room held guests in a vice-like grip, as dinners became ritualized theatre, while the apse of the reception room framed the *dominus* as mini-emperor. Using A.H.M. Jones' work on late Roman municipal governance, Ellis further argued that the proliferation of reception and dining spaces were a product of previously civic functions – judicial courts, municipal politics, even church services – making their way into domestic space. In cities in which many houses were abandoned or subdivided for multi-family living and in which the physical apparatus of civic life –

1. Inventing the Later Roman House

the forum, the basilicas, the *curia* – was crumbling, the increasing splendour of a few large houses signalled the takeover of municipal functions by a narrow group of elites (Ellis 1988, 573-5; 1991, 123; 1997b, 46-7, cf. Jones 1964, 2: 737-63). The late Roman house thus witnessed the replacement of participatory politics with the closed-door dealings of the powerful few.

Ellis' careful collation of spatial topographies with social context has influenced a whole generation of recent studies, both conceptual and regionally-organized, often alongside revivals of the earlier 'imperial' model (Sfameni 2006b, 178-9; Scott 2004, 52-3; Tione 1999; Özgenel 2007; Waelkens et al. 2007, 502-3). Federico Guidobaldi's seminal studies on the urban *domus* of Rome assume that locally available imperial models – the Palatine palaces in particular – heavily influenced the forms and ideology of later houses, like the so-called House of the Valerii on the Caelian (Fig. 9), or the many apsed audience halls discovered beneath the city's churches (Guidobaldi 1986, 220, 228; 1993, 73; 1999, 57-9). Citing the absence of evidence for new apartment, or *insula*, construction and the conversion of some *insulae* into large, elite *domus*, Guidobaldi weds an emphasis on imperial trend-setting with a version of Ellis' paradigm: the absence of the emperors in fourth-century Rome allowed the senatorial aristocracy to assume their place, and the expansion of the elite *domus* at the expense of multifamily housing and civic projects marked the takeover of urban affairs by the aristocracy.

Isabella Baldini-Lippolis' pan-Mediterranean survey of the urban *domus*, on the other hand, eschews any discussion of urban politics, and re-emphasizes instead the strongly hierarchical, even ritualized comportment produced through these houses' succession of special nuclei. Its origins, she claims, lay in the imperial palaces of the late third and early fourth centuries, which constituted a homogeneous imperial system (Baldini Lippolis 2002, 47, 49, 53, 109-11). This architecture was copied by senatorial elites as their own social relationships mirrored the hierarchization and ritualization manifest in the

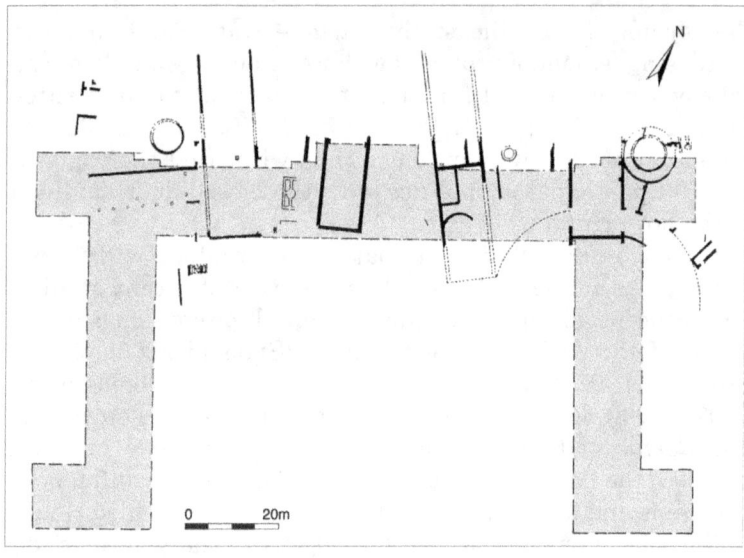

Fig. 9. House of the Valerii, Rome.

late antique court, and in which emperor, and by imitation the *dominus*, sought to appear larger than life.

Some of the most detailed recent examinations of houses and society have focused on rural villas in the provinces – Aquitaine, Britain, Hispania, Italy, and the Danubian provinces (e.g. Scott 2000; Balmelle 2001; Mulvin 2002; Sfmanei 2006b; Chavarría 2007). Most of these studies eschew direct imperial models and rely on conceptions of rural hierarchies as their explanatory mechanism. Through the villa, the *dominus* maintained hawk-like vigilance over his inferior tenants by making his power manifest in soaring spaces and sparkling mosaics, like those at Carranque or Piazza Armerina (see Figs 5 & 2-3), and by centralizing rent collection and agricultural processing in that same venue (Chavarría 2007, 53; Sfameni 2006b, 20-2, 175-7. Balmelle, 2001, 55-64, is more cautious). Many of these studies have been at pains to reject the earlier assumption that the proliferation of rural residences was the result of declining civic participation, a so-called 'ruralization' produced by civic

1. Inventing the Later Roman House

elites fleeing municipal responsibilities (Chavarría 2007, 112; Sfameni 2006b, 165-89; cf. Scott 2000, 106-7; 2004, 41-4, who retains the notion of urban flight). The senatorial elite, or *clarissimi*, are the posited protagonists: 'self-display', through personalized mosaic inscriptions and eclectic statue collections, helped unite this class, while the proliferation of apsed reception spaces and expansive entrance courtyards reiterated their supremacy over their inferiors (Balmelle 2001, 37-48; Sfameni 2006b, 141-6, 183-5; Chavarría 2007, 41-2; 112-13; 2005, 539-44). For many scholars, the late Roman villa marked this senatorial elite's increasing emphasis on their private affairs in the face of their reduced role in imperial politics, which a heavy reliance on the personal letters of the senator Symmachus seems to support. Sharp, domineering patronage, over provincial inferiors and over their own tenants, was the principal preoccupation of these landed *clarissimi*, and required the hierarchical spaces of reception and dining halls (Chavarría 2007, 67, 113; Sfameni 2006b, 183-7; 2006a; Scott 2000, 106-7; 110-11; cf. Balmelle 2001, 43-4).

This brief overview does not pretend to be complete, or to do justice to the nuance of individual arguments which vary in detail and emphasis. I hope it does convey three salient points. First, the subject's origins in medieval architectural history have exerted a significant impact on its later socio-historical developments. Apses, axiality and other properties were originally read through the backward lens of church architecture, and later social analyses often attributed to these forms a functional and ideological meaning – ritual and hierarchy – informed by their Christian uses. This early history similarly positioned these houses in a medieval-oriented teleology in which their 'difference' from previous Roman houses was fundamental to the development of 'new' architectural, and ultimately social, forms. The periodized 'late antique house' is in part traceable to these early studies and more recent work has yet to shake off its now tacit influence.

Second, contrary to recent work on earlier ancient houses, the study of late antique houses has been and continues to be strongly influenced by textually-derived models of social history. The notion of 'ritualized' comportment – be it of imperial ceremonies or elite dinner parties – is derived from sources like Ammianus Marcellinus' description of the emperor Constantinius II's ceremonial arrival into Rome or Sidonius Apollinaris' description of party *placement* (Ammianus Marcellinus 16.10; Sidonius Apollinaris, *Letters* 1.11.10-17). The replacement of civic government with a narrow band of grandees ensconced in urban super-*domus* is lamented by the orator Libanius, while the Christian critic Salvian heaps scorn on the villas of the powerful that presided over the oppression of the rural poor. Scholars have read these texts directly onto houses or applied them through the filter of secondary historical paradigms. That is, unlike its sister disciplines in classical Greek and earlier Roman house studies, the study of later Roman houses remains firmly tethered to texts.

Owing to both its medieval-oriented teleologies and its strong reliance on textual histories, the recent work on the late antique house has been dominated by one interpretative paradigm – hierarchization. Late Roman houses, be they urban *domus* or rural villas, are thought to be the product of a precipitously hierarchical culture in which the spaces of dining and reception separated dinners with peers from meetings with inferiors. The great rural villas were the centrepieces of much larger estates and their splendid halls the status-markers of the confident few who dominated the socially-distant many, while the great urban *domus* hosted judicial courts, embassies and other municipal activities, taking the place of a crumbling civic apparatus. Hierarchization, ritualization and privatization are the buzz-words that embody a particularly 'late antique' kind of house.

The following chapters examine in detail the evidence upon which this paradigm is based and the methodologies that shape its use. They suggest that a tendency to read social history onto archaeology has lead archaeologists to ignore the very different evidence of the archaeology itself. When stripped of *a priori* historical assumptions, that archaeology provides little sup-

1. Inventing the Later Roman House

port for the narrative outlined above. In their spatial layouts and functional distributions, later Roman houses look very much like the houses of the earlier empire, while their innovations cannot be interpreted as producing particularly 'hierarchical' or 'ritual' spatial behaviours. Additionally, the socio-historical models that have been read onto these houses are largely out of date and have been succeeded by studies that offer more nuanced readings of the primary sources and, like the archaeology, emphasize the strong continuities with earlier Roman social relationships.

2

The Archaeology of Later Roman Houses

Over the last decade, an effort to collect and catalogue all extant late Roman houses has had a number of salubrious effects (e.g. Balmelle 2001; Baldini Lipollis 2002; Chavarría 2007; Sfameni 2006b; Bullo and Ghedini 2003), not least exposing the limitations of the evidence, and how those qualitative defects have shaped interpretative paradigms. The most significant limitation is chronological; much of the corpus consists of houses excavated early in the century, often without careful recording or attention to phasing and stratigraphy. The dating of many such houses is based on style of mosaic floors or the presence of apses, and they are often assigned broad 'late antique' dates. New open-area excavations have revealed how misleading these broad chronologies can be: houses often evolved on generational rather than epochal time frames, the product of individual, often quixotic interventions rather than lock-step responses to 'society'. Illustrative is the so-called Triconch Palace in Butrint, Albania (see Fig. 4), whose plan would appear to present a typical late antique house with apsed halls and separated reception spaces. However, careful stratigraphic excavation has revealed near-constant third- to early fifth-century spatial alterations, many of which failed to function in concert. The project culminated in early fifth-century additions, including a massive triconch dining room, which were never completed (Gilkes and Lako 2004; Bowden and Mitchell 2007; Bowden forthcoming). That is, the 'typical' late antique house plan is here revealed to be an incomplete palimpsest. The 'late antique' character of houses broadly

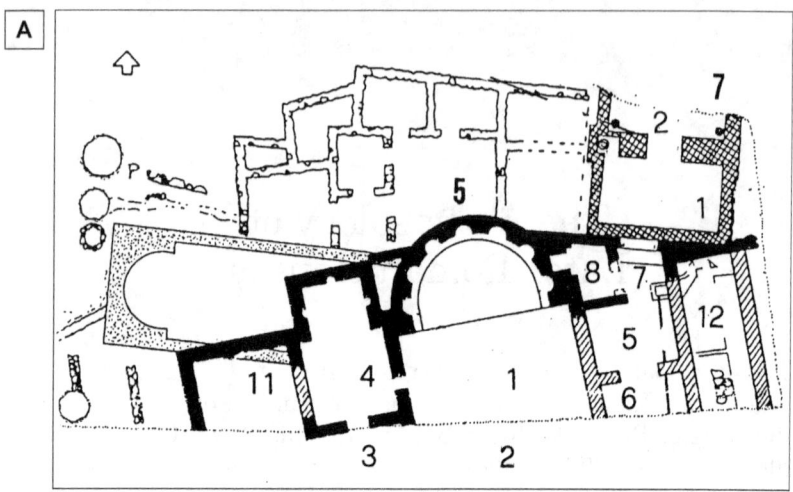

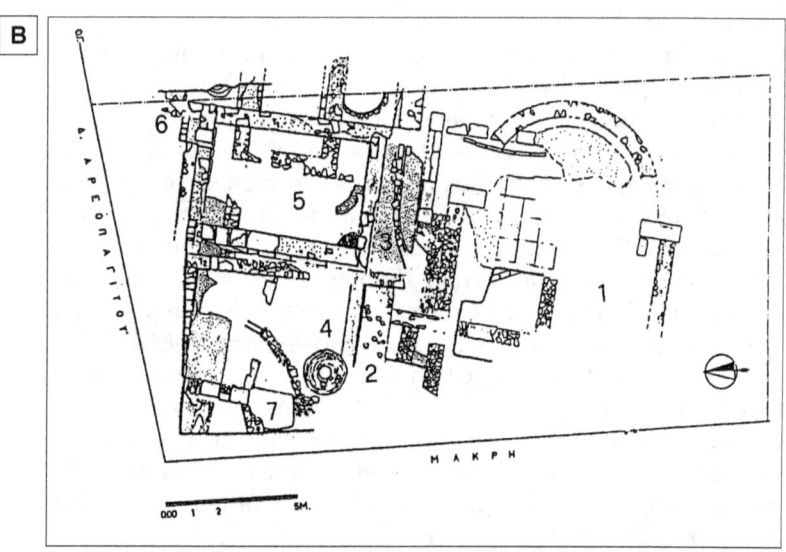

Fig. 10. House plans from Athens. A: House of Proclus; B: House between Dyonisiou Areopagitou and Makri Streets; C (*opposite*): House between Irodou Attikou 2 and Basilissis Sofias Streets.

2. The Archaeology of Later Roman Houses

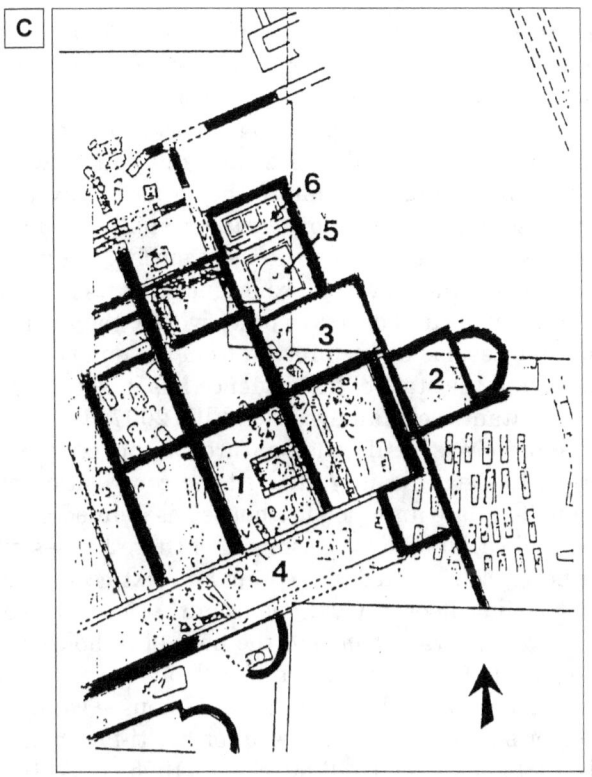

dated to 'late antiquity' thus runs the risk of being somewhat self-determined.

Given the lacunose state of much of the archaeological corpus, plans are often the only tool remaining for re-analysis. But the plans themselves are often only partial, particularly in urban contexts. Analysis of house plans, for instance those of Rome or Athens, has proceeded using only partially-excavated or preserved houses (Fig. 10), and thus without any clear indication of entrances, house boundaries or interfaces with surrounding buildings (Guidobaldi 1986; Frantz 1988, respectively). Upper storeys, as a new study has suggested, became important living and reception spaces in this period and often are just as significantly erased (Polci 2003). Moreover, houses excavated without modern methods (the majority of the corpus) were stripped, often without documentation, of their accompanying artifacts. Although artistic finds such as sculpture were typically recorded in early excavation reports, ceramics, bone and other materials typically were not, and thus any living surfaces, and the invaluable glimpse they afford of lived experience, are absent. As noted above, artifact analysis on earlier Roman houses gives a sense of what those surfaces might have revealed – the messiness of lived experience and its defiance of patterns set by walls and doors. In other words, the analysis of late Roman houses has had to proceed from the empty shells of such houses, and the state of the evidence has inevitably influenced the resultant social analyses (cf. Ellis 2007, 3).

The planar versus artifactual nature of the late antique house corpus has significantly affected the composition of the corpus itself. The 'late antique elite house', as defined by many catalogues and social analyses, consists of those houses which are either newly constructed in the fourth to sixth centuries, or show major wall or floor renovations from that period. Indeed, according to one prevalent model, the only elite houses occupied in late antiquity consisted of such heavily renovated or newly built structures, while all other elite houses were either abandoned, or subdivided and re-used for multi-family habitation (Ellis 1988, 565; 1997b, 46-50; Sodini 1995; 1997; Baldini Lippolis 2002). That is, late antique houses, and by extension late antique elites, represented a narrow, homogeneous band of extraordinary wealth, beneath which lay an equally undifferentiated poor. Left out of this model, and most corpora, are older elite houses that were maintained as such, but had no recognizable mural additions. Detecting continued maintenance and elite occupation requires stratigraphic archaeology and contextual reporting often absent in early excavations, but increasingly available in new studies. The modest but proudly decorated fourth-century apartments in Hanghaus 1 at Ephesus (Fig. 11), the large and small elite houses of the Morería in Mérida, the continued maintenance of some villas of the Roman *suburbium* – all show signs of pretension, most

2. The Archaeology of Later Roman Houses

are typically omitted from studies of the late Roman house, and all describe precisely the kind of occupation that late antiquity is said to lack – the deep substrata of more modest elites (Lang-Auinger 1996, 92-119; 204-6; Alba Calzado 1997; Volpe 2003, 218-29, respectively). Similarly, the large corpus of finely-built houses from the Syrian villages is rarely considered in overall assessments of 'the late antique house', yet they provide ample evidence for the houses of the aspiring rural elite (Brown 1971). In other words, owing to its previously lacunose, or highly selective archaeology, our perception of elite houses has been potentially skewed towards houses which have recognizably late antique mural elements, that is, houses that look different, and probably houses at the top end of the socio-economic scale. Potentially undercounted are old houses or houses which, like the grammarians or imperial bureaucrats of the age, were 'respectable, but unprepossessing' (Kelly 2004, 151, quoting Kaster 1988, 99-134). To miss these would be to miss the brownstones of modern New York City or the Victorian renovations in San Francisco and judge twentieth-century housing on Frank Lloyd Wright alone. While quite understandable in purely architectural studies, it presents an obvious problem to those interested in the social qualities of houses.

The most distinctive qualities of late antique houses are thought to lie in the differential emphasis and arrangement of interior space. Enlarged and elaborated *triclinia* are said to demonstrate a ritualization of banquets; larger, apsed audience halls (termed *aulae*, 'basilicas' or 'reception rooms' in the secondary literature) indicate civic activities enfolded into the private sphere; while the separation of these dining and reception halls demonstrates social separation and hierarchization. Some have even concluded that late Roman houses thus saw greater functional separation between 'public' and 'private' spaces than did their predecessors (Ellis 1991, 123; Thébert 1987, 389-91). It is in these functionally-specific rooms, and particularly in their spatial separation, that the defining aspects of the late Roman house are generally thought to lie.

Houses and Society in the Later Roman Empire

As described in the previous chapter, room-based 'functionalism' has come under fire from students of ancient domestic architecture, whose recent work on Pompeian and Greek housing has undermined the notion that form, or even location within the home, is a reliable indicator of function. Artifact analysis has further suggested that, with the exception of rooms with fixed installations like kitchens and latrines, house spaces were generally multifunctional; dining rooms might be used for sleeping and cooking; reception rooms might be used for storage (Allison 1997; 2006; Berry 1997; Ault and Nevett 1999). Few late antique houses have been excavated with sufficient care to find the rare remnants of living levels and their artifacts, and many that have preserve only the latest levels, often from periods after the houses' use as elite habitations. Nonetheless, the few recent results, seemingly reflective of third to early sixth-century realities, are interesting. A large

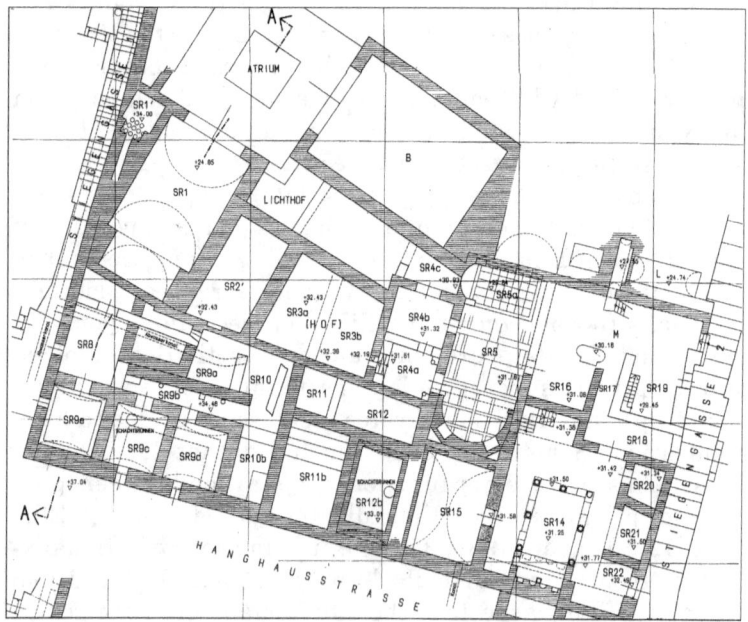

Fig. 11. Hanghaus 1, Ephesus, Turkey, late fourth-century phase.

2. The Archaeology of Later Roman Houses

suburban *domus* in Sagalassos (Turkey) saw an intimate 'private' courtyard used for amphora storage, seemingly before the building's slow demise in the mid-sixth century (Putzeys et al. 2004). Similarly, at Xanthos (Syria) a room identified as a 'tablinum' owing to its decoration and location, was filled with storage amphorae and dolia, again seemingly from a living surface prior to the room's conversion into a sheepfold (Manière-Levêque 2007, 479-82). The new phasing in the multilevel townhouse known as Hanghaus 2 at Ephesus has revealed similar finds from mid-third-century destruction levels: Kapitan II amphorae leaned against the vestibule walls, cultic objects, work tools and cooking pots littered a fine forecourt, graffiti celebrated a summer dinner outside in the courtyard, while an upper-story 'representation' room paved with mosaic was littered with a hoe and amphorae as well as sculpture fragments (Ladstätter 2005, 252, 243; Jilek 2005, 389, 400, 403; Thür 2005, 417, 420-1) (Fig. 12). It is slight evidence as yet, but the multifunctionality evident in Greek and earlier Roman houses, suggestive of wildly diverse activities inside single spaces, probably also characterized later houses.

The social implications are potentially significant: if one cannot identify with certainty a dining room, reception room or other room type from architecture or location alone, and if these spaces admitted a variety of functions depending on time of day and personal whim of the inhabitants, the link between architectural form and function is weakened. Thus, the tendency to interpret domestic architecture through individual socially-pregnant functions – dining or reception – becomes methodologically suspect. In particular, if dining and reception rooms admitted a variety of functions, the presumed functional segregation of reception spaces produced by social hierarchization likewise becomes hard to sustain. Indeed, the alleged capacity of late antique houses to successfully separate different classes of people and activities is similarly undermined if such rooms were littered with workman's tools or amphorae from a recent delivery. It may be that later Roman houses were

Houses and Society in the Later Roman Empire

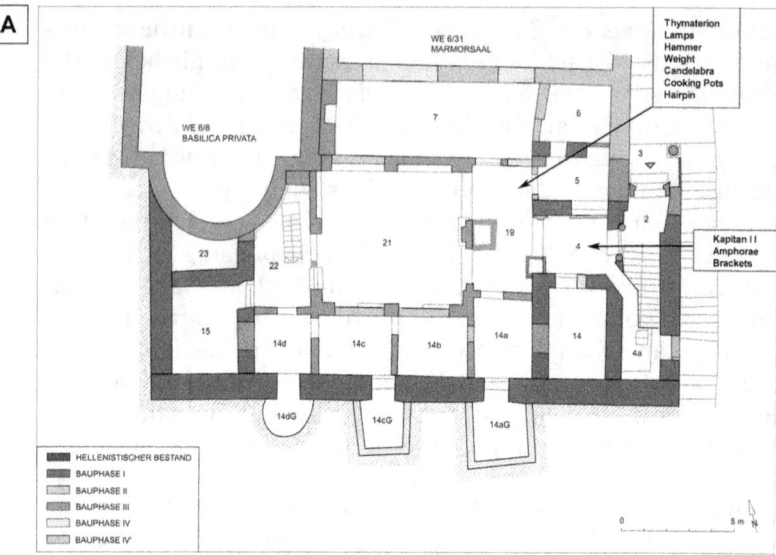

Fig. 12. Hanghaus 2.4, Ephesus, Turkey, mid-third-century phase plans with find assemblages. A: lower floor. B (*opposite*): upper floor.

more socio-functionally determined than their predecessors, but the burden of proof must lie with the archaeologists, through artifact assemblage studies, to prove such a shift. This they have not yet done (cf. Perring 2003, 701-4).

Social control and public/private in the late Roman house

There are other reasons to doubt that functional and hierarchical spatial separation really took place in late antique houses. The separation of a street-side 'reception' room from an interior 'dining room', documented in a series of eastern and North African urban houses, was central to Ellis' hypothesis of social segregation and increased hierarchization (Ellis 1988, 569-70; 1997a, 120-3; 1997b, 46-7). It has profoundly influenced the study of all later Roman houses, whether or not they exhibit this combination (Baldini Lippolis 2002, 47; Ghedini 2003, vol.

2. The Archaeology of Later Roman Houses

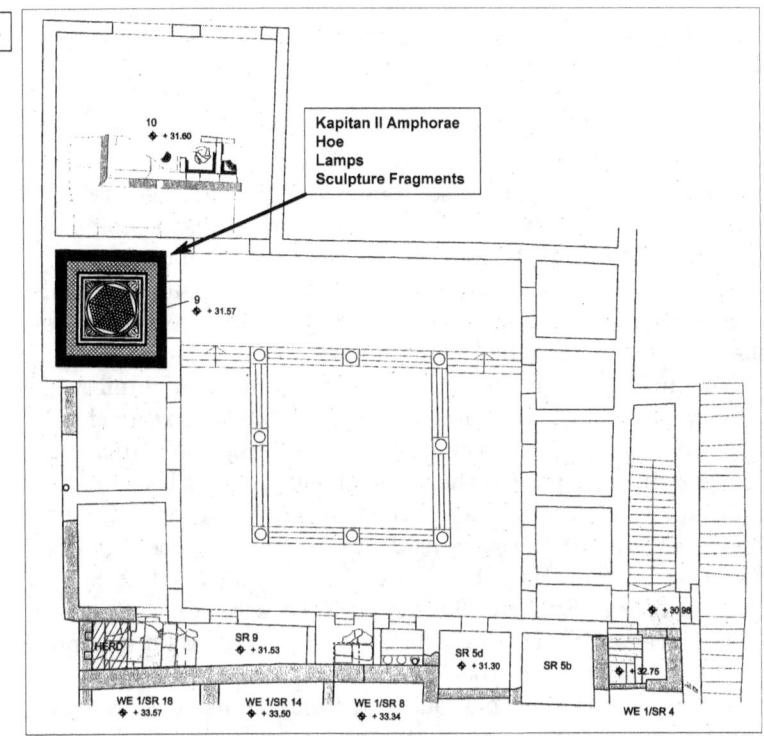

1, 343). For instance, a recent study of Asia Minor houses has produced a series of house plans with assigned room function based on Ellis' model, while the recent excellent excavations of a late town house at Sagalassos have similarly not only identified separate 'reception' and 'dining rooms' from spaces which show no decoration or are only partially preserved, but seem to have taken the further step of reconstructing the house's circulation patterns, which are nowhere clear due to later rebuilding and poor preservation (Özgenel 2007; Waelkens et al. 2007). While students of rural villas have noted that reception/*triclinium* separation is rare in rural examples, the social implications derived from such separation – social segregation, vertiginous patronage relationships, etc. – are nonetheless often applied to the interpretations of these spaces (Scott 2000, 108; Mulvin 2002, 40; Sfameni 2006b, 178-9).

Leaving aside the problematic functionalist identification of such rooms as 'dining rooms' or 'reception rooms', comprehensive catalogues of late antique houses have now made it possible to be more precise about what constituted 'typical' spatial arrangements. Grand entrance complexes are common, particularly in rural villas where space was abundant (e.g. Balmelle 2001, 152-5; Chavarría 2007, 95). Multiple, highly decorated rooms off a central peristyle are also common, as they had been since the late republic.

But among the many hundreds of urban *domus* and rural villas with major late Roman phases, only about six can clearly be shown to have a separated street-side 'reception' hall and an interior 'dining' space of the type Ellis identified. These are, at Aphrodisias (Turkey), the so-called Bishop's House (Fig. 13); at Apollonia (Libya), the so-called House of the Dux (see Fig. 1); at Bulla Regia (Tunisia), the House of the Hunt (see Fig. 8) and House No. 3; at Ephesus (Turkey), the Theatre House (Fig. 14); and at Fraga (Spain), the Villa Fortunatus (see Baldini Lippolis 2002, 119, 142-4, 165-6; Keil 1932; Thür 2002b, 257-64; Navarro Sáez 1999). The houses at Stobi, House of Peristeria, and Xanthos, Northeast House, may be read this way, but it is less clear (see Baldini Lippolis 2002, 300; Manière-Lévêque 2007, respectively). At the villa of Nérac in Aquitaine, two back-to-back entrance apsed halls have been unearthed, but the rest of the residential area and its layout remains unexcavated (Balmelle 2001, 390-3). Other examples are included in Özgenel's study of Asia Minor houses but do not display the near-door reception and interior *triclinium* arrangement proposed by Ellis, either because the proposed 'audience room' is located well inside the *domus*, or because separate dining/reception spaces have not been located.

Whether so small a number can be said to represent a trend is doubtful, while the social-historical interpretations derived from this small sample now appear to be overstated, given that they fail to explain the vast majority of examples. Further-

2. The Archaeology of Later Roman Houses

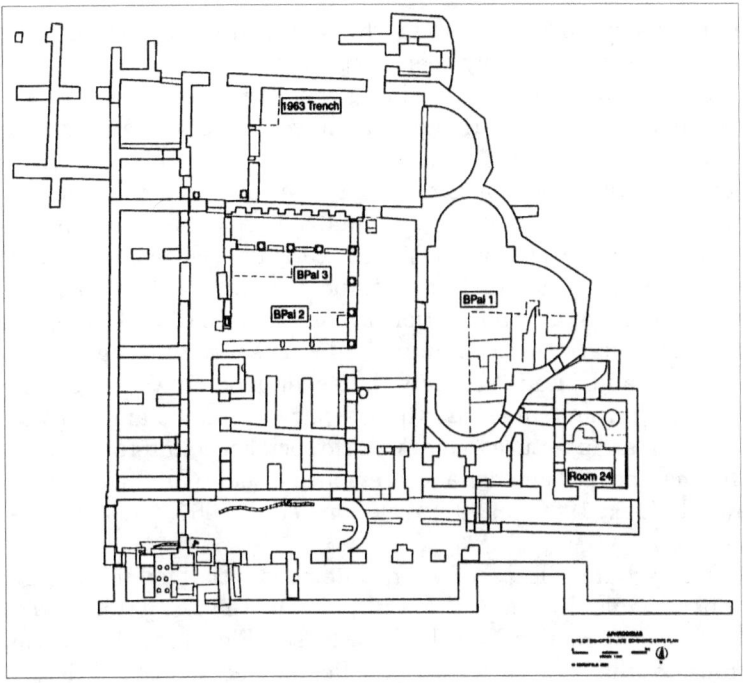

Fig. 13. Bishop's House, Aphrodisias.

more, of this corpus, only two can be shown to be definitive products of a single-phase of new construction – the Bishops' House in Aphrodisias and the Palace of the Dux. The other four houses have major earlier phases which saw the construction of so-called 'triclinia', while the street-side 'reception halls' were seemingly added in late antiquity. Another cautionary tale is provided by the careful excavations at the Triconch Palace in Butrint: here a lateral apsed hall and triconch seem to fit the pattern, but the phasing reveals a palimpsest of rapid planar changes in which the apsed hall had already been marginalized – by new buildings cutting off the entrance and an ugly drain cut through its access corridor – at the time when the triconch was added (Bowden and Mitchell 2007, 458-66) (see Fig. 4). Thus, most late antique houses, it is now clear, did not have spatially separate venues for socially distinct groups and thus the notion of social 'hierarchization' based on that separation has probably been exaggerated.

In addition to reception/dining separation, late antique urban houses are also thought to have witnessed an altered articulation of 'public' and 'private' space. In this view, the single, distributive space of peristyle or atrium in earlier Roman houses made all rooms equally permeable – a kind of spatial democratization – while the corridors, closing walls and separate entrances of late antique houses are said to have separated 'private' habitation areas from the 'public' representative quarters. Even individual rooms were no longer open to views and public scrutiny, but ever more inward-looking. The late antique *dominus* thus 'separated public and private and used architecture to manipulate social encounters in a way that had never been done in previous periods' (Ellis 1991, 123; also Thébert 1987, 389-91; Waelkens et al. 2007, 502-3, Ghedini 2003, 343).

Thébert and Ellis' studies include houses that exhibit highly impermeable rooms – the Aphrodisias Bishops' House *triclinium* is screened by a high wall (see Fig. 8), while at the House of the New Hunt in Bulla Regia, pieces of the peristyle were enfolded into new room groupings (see Fig. 14). But does this represent a significant shift in public/private topographies? Again, such claims seem to be rooted less in a careful diachronic study of access and permeability, which these studies lack, and more in a caricatured periodization of both early and late houses – the late republican house was open and 'public', the late Roman house was closed and 'private'. (e.g. Ellis 1991, 122-3). These claims should be considered against the age-old tension of public and private which marks Roman houses of all periods (e.g. Riggsby 1997; Sessa 2007). Andrew Wallace-Hadrill's conception of an intersecting spectrum of public/private, grand/humble spaces in Pompeian houses not only highlighted the overlap of 'public' and 'private' in such houses, but pointed just as insistently to the extremes of permeable/impermeable within in a single house, from the permeable atrium/*tablinum* combination to the impermeable,

2. The Archaeology of Later Roman Houses

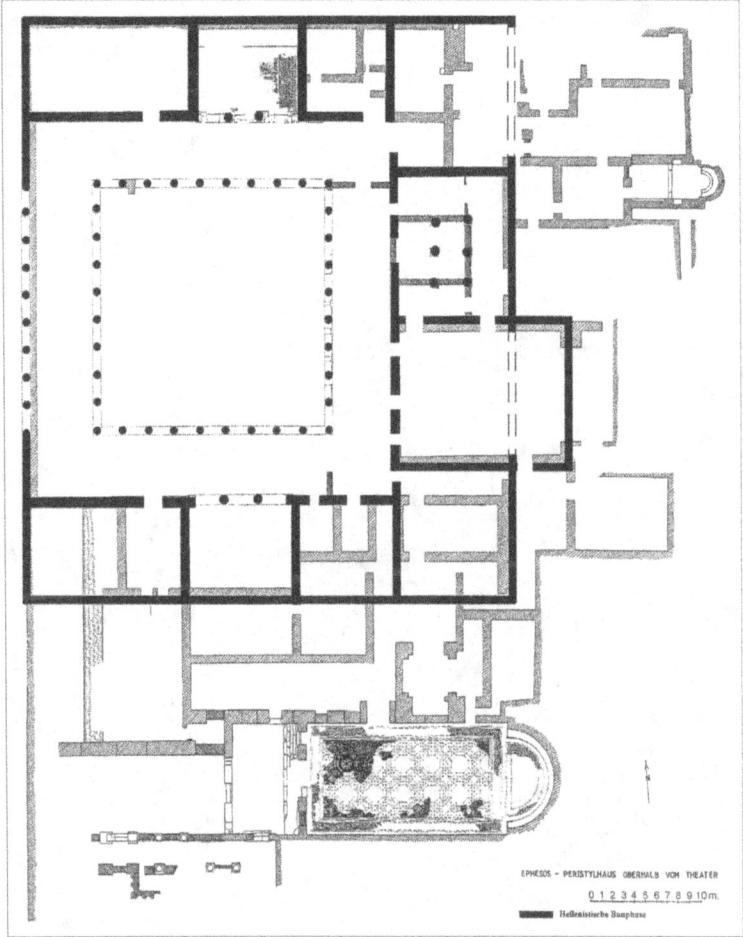

Fig. 14. Theatre House, Ephesus, Turkey, showing Hellenistic (black) and late antique (grey) phases.

secondary mini-atrium surrounded by *cubicula* (Wallace-Hadrill 1994, 11, 17-37). Three-dimensional analyses reveal further nuances. As a more recent study suggests, Pompeian houses engage in deliberate 'fake-outs', providing tantalizing views of spaces to which they ultimately forbid or limit access: vision

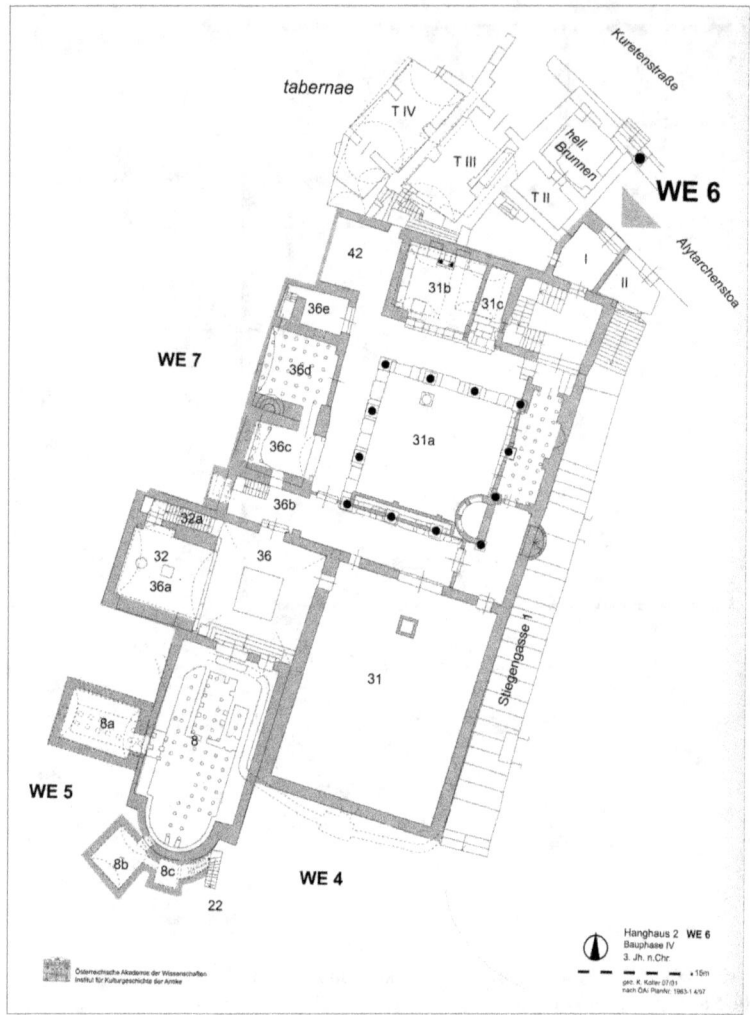

Fig. 15. Hanghaus 2.6, Ephesus, third-century phase.

and access might thus produce different 'maps' of public and private (Hales 2003, 107-22). Such tensions are similarly visible in the public/private topographies of other regions' houses, which seem to persist over the *longue durée*. For instance, later

2. The Archaeology of Later Roman Houses

second-century modifications to Hanghaus 2.6 in Ephesus created two separated reception spaces, one on the peristyle and a second apsed hall set apart, off a separate atrium (Thür 2002a, 60-3) (Fig. 15). The result resembles a dining/reception separation supposedly characteristic of late antique houses, but a century earlier. Similarly, the second-century houses at Volubilis (Morocco) display radically different access patterns – shielding the main house down circuitous corridors (as at the Maison aux demi-Colonnes), or making it visible through axial alignments linking entrance to reception space (as in the Maison à l'Ouest du Palais du Gouverneur) (Etienne 1960; Hales 2003, 198) (Fig. 16).

When phased chronologies are considered and the full range of available evidence is brought to bear, the same range of 'public' and 'private' spaces and the same diverse approaches to encouraging and limiting access are found in the houses of the late empire. For instance, in the fourth-/fifth-century modifications to houses at Djemila (Tunisia), a side entrance and long corridors were preserved and elaborated through many phases at the Maison d'Europe, producing an enclosed, inward looking house, while the axial grandiosity at the Maison de Bacchus was amplified over time (Blanchard-Lemée 1975, 129-51; 1981, 131-41) (Fig. 17). A new survey of Tunisian houses has likewise revealed the great variety of access and permeability, variety which seems to have no real chronological periodicity, even as the author repeats the claim that later houses exhibit increasing patterns of social distinction (Ghedini 2003, 318-34).

Finally, Thébert had interpreted dividing walls and other signs of compartmentalization as indicative of an increasing desire for 'privacy' and/or to screen and separate the elite from their inferiors (Thébert 1987, 389-90). In some cases, these dividing walls may post-date the elite occupation of the house, perhaps by as much as some centuries, and probably belong to later phases in which these houses were subdivided into multi-family habitations. This phenomenon has seen important study in its own right (Brogiolo and Gelichi 1998; Chavarría 2007, 157-9), but it is probably distinct, both in social aspect and chronology, from the 'elite' phases of these *domus*. The other examples cited by Thébert – the low walls between the columns of the peristyle or the annexation of portico space as vestibules for other rooms in the House of the New Hunt (see top of Fig. 8) – doubtless reconfigured the spatial dynamics, fragmenting their sightlines. The social implications of these changes, however, are multiple, and the notion that they were solely and necessarily a product of a more hierarchical society or one preoccupied with 'modesty', seems driven more by *a priori* assumptions about that society than any consistent properties of the spaces themselves. In sum, the notion that late antique houses exhibited greater public/private distinction and separa-

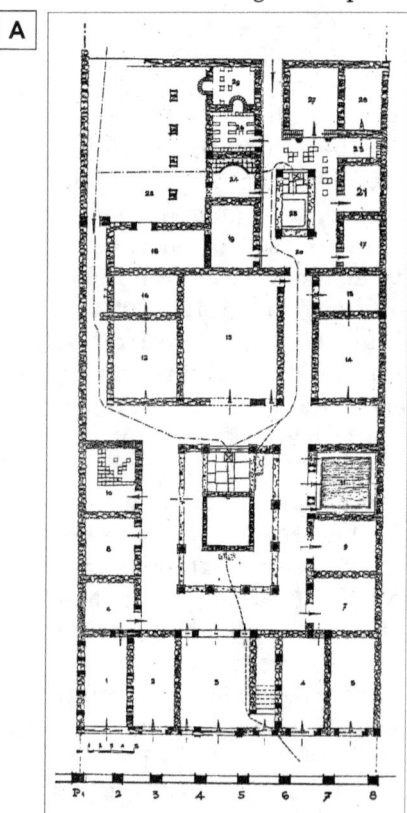

Fig. 16. A: Maison à l'Ouest du Palais du Gouverneur; B (*opposite*): Maison aux demi-Colonnes, Volubilis, Morocco.

2. The Archaeology of Later Roman Houses

tion is hard to sustain; more apparent is a continued exploitation of the public/private spectrum in its infinite variation.

The absorption of 'public' architectural elements – the apsidal hall and private baths being the most remarked-upon – should similarly be regarded within the long and ever-shifting relationship between domestic and civic architecture. As Wallace-Hadrill has emphasized, even the most financially-strapped Pompeians were at pains to integrate an allusion to civic life – tiny colonnades, cityscape paintings – into their homes (Wallace-Hadrill 1994, 17-37). The embrace of the longitudinal, apsidal hall by late antique homeowners, urban and rural, should be also seen in this continuum (see for instance Figs 1, 2, 13, 15). Students of late Roman houses have been understandably gripped by the parallels between the apsed, aisleless 'audience halls' of their subjects, and those of the imperial Flavian Palace in Rome, where the form (with narrow

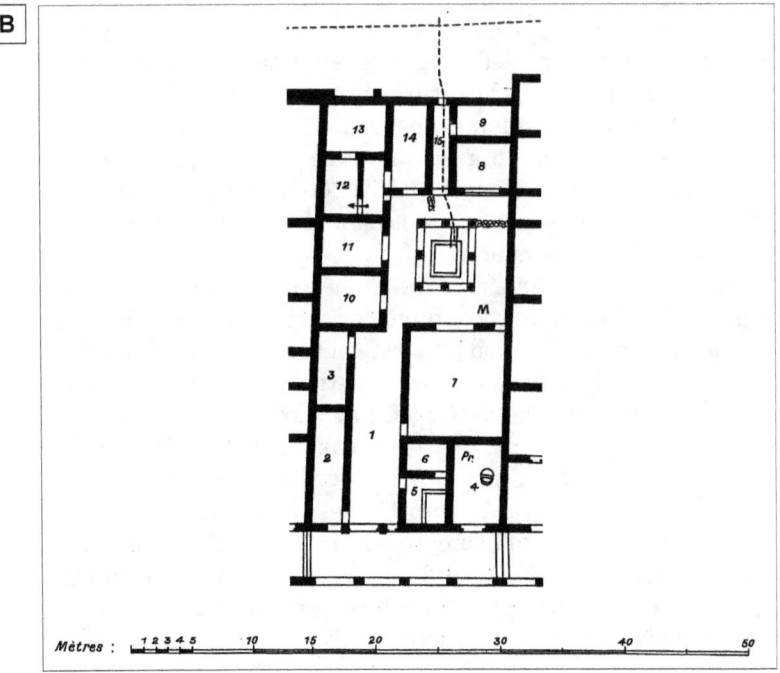

B

Houses and Society in the Later Roman Empire

aisles) made its first major appearance in the domestic sphere to showcase the semi-divine properties of the emperor (Baldini Lippolis 2002, 29-30; Ellis 1991, 119; cf. Krautheimer 1969, 12-13; Ward-Perkins 1954). As many have noted, two centuries separated the completion of the latter and the proliferation of the former, and in the meantime, the concrete revolution of the second century AD ushered in a new face for later Roman civic architecture, one in which the apsed hall played a major role. The increasing use of apses as capstones for longitudinal rooms, and of exedrae and other curvilinear forms to break spatial confines, marked the development of judicial basilicas, temples, baths and nymphea, as well as imperial audience halls (Ward-Perkins 1974, 100-1, 415-28; Tamm 1963, 147-88; Schweizer 2005). The apsed hall, in other words, was no longer monopolized by the imperial person, and its spread to baths and libraries, not to mention the multifunctional reception/dining rooms, diluted its signification well beyond monolithic ideas of majesty. If it carried any particularized meaning, the apse would have signalled a generalized notion of 'the civic' and of that urban public architecture through which it had spread (Ćurčić 1993). Just as new elites of the first and second centuries AD had seized upon a flexible idea of 'basilican' forms to announce their civic belonging (Gros 2004), the domestic apsed hall finds later homeowners quoting a recognizable, but highly malleable, civic vocabulary.

Domestic bath complexes, which Thébert attributed to elites' desire for seclusion and avoidance of social inferiors, likewise have a long and variegated history, going in and out of popularity, and similarly defy easy categorization as the 'privatization' of a previously 'public' activity (cf. Fabbricotti 1976). While the majority of North African private baths studied by Thébert are fourth-century in date, this coincides with the differential preservation of most North African houses, whose fourth-century phases are the best, and sometimes the only, phases manifest (Thébert 2003, 368; Ghiotto 2003, 221-32). More remarkable than their date, however, is their highly-regional demographic. Overall, private bath construction remained relatively rare: of

2. The Archaeology of Later Roman Houses

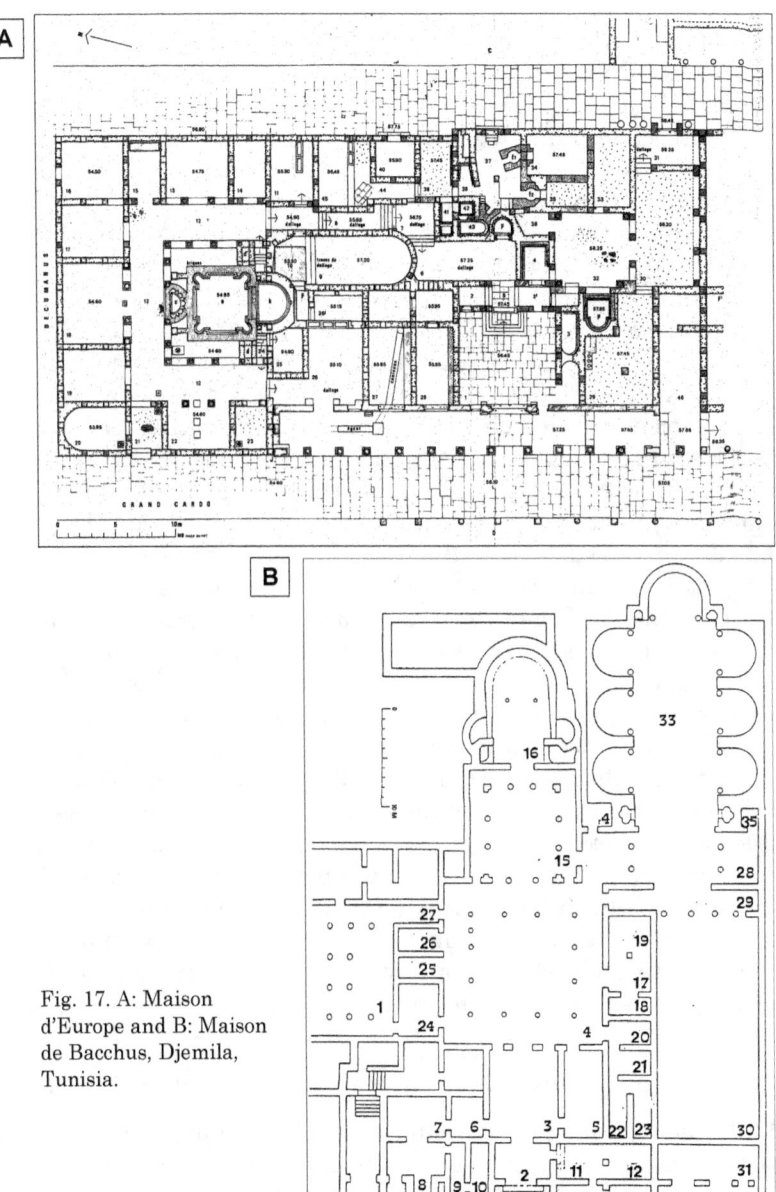

Fig. 17. A: Maison d'Europe and B: Maison de Bacchus, Djemila, Tunisia.

the 136 houses included in a recent Tunisian survey, only 5.9% had baths (Ghiotto 2003, 227). Many cities rich in late antique houses, like Thugga, produced few or no domestic baths, while other cities like Bulla Regia had a half-dozen or more (Thébert 2003, 363) (see Fig. 8). Far from representing a general social imperative, private bath-building seems to have been a local choice. Furthermore, many of the North African *domus*-baths Thébert studied have two entrances – one from the *domus* itself, and a second large, street-side door, the latter possibly for the use of non-householders (cf. Ghiotto 2003, 226-7). Far from shying away from the urban crush, they seem to invite it into the home. Finally, and as will be discussed below, the elaboration of private baths in these North African cities saw no widespread abandonment of the public baths (Lepelley 1979-81, 295-6; Thébert 2003, 415-18). Thus there is no reason to assume that private bath construction was due to a rejection of the public baths, any more than there is to think that first-century AD Pompeians refrained from public bathing in favour of their many private baths (see Fagan 1999, 63-4). Indeed, the characterization of *domus*-bathing as 'private' and civic bathing as 'public' fails to take into account the many domestic baths-for-profit, or public bathing made private by the human shield of servants – that is, the inherent resistance of Roman bathing to conform to easy public/private dichotomies (Fagan 1999, 65-8,123-7; 206-19).

In short, the notion of 'privatization' in late antique homes, at least as regards the appropriation of apsed halls and domestic baths, rests on a simplified, often periodized conception of the private, which seems less persuasive when viewed in a more complex, diachronic light. Instead, it is the continued reference to and reliance on civic life and its architectural forms which seem more noteworthy.

Dining and apses: the shock of the new

While one may reject a particularized 'late antique' public/private domestic topography, other domestic architectural developments seem genuinely new. The most apparent is the

2. The Archaeology of Later Roman Houses

proliferation of the apse. As a mode of referencing civic architecture, the apse formed part of a long continuum; the curvilinear form of that quotation, however, was a particularly late antique phenomenon. Even taking into account a certain tendency to assign *a priori* late Roman dates to any apsed forms, the preponderance of apses in late Roman houses is indisputable. Indeed, they appear with some rapidity, absent in the Severan Marble Plan for instance, and present in both elite and modest Roman city *domus* a century later, a trend which is echoed in the cities and villas of the provinces (Guidobaldi 1986, 20). The proliferation of the apse thus changed the aesthetics and spatial character of houses in large and small ways.

We have already suggested a generalized association of apsidal halls with new forms of civic architecture. Its appearance in spaces identified as dining rooms, however, is thought to have additional meanings, where it is associated with the later Roman advent of the *stibadium*, or semi-circular dining couch. Ellis has further suggested that the paired apse/*stibadium* development either produced, or was produced by, an increasing rigidity in dining behaviour. The portable couches of earlier *triclinia* were replaced by permanent semi-circular couches, rendering dining rooms unusable for any other purpose (Ellis 1997a). The confining space of the apse, often raised above the rest of the room, rendered movement difficult and thus hierarchies more rigid. The result was a, 'greater ritualisation and formalisation of entertainment' (Ellis 1997a, 51).

The formal resemblance between these apsed dining rooms and later church architecture, and the early historiography that read apses as products of ritual (e.g. Lavin 1962; Dyggve 1961; L'Orange 1965, 79-83), has perhaps made this notion of 'ritualization' more persuasive than it should be. Permanent masonry *stibadia* are quite rare – only about ten extant examples – as rare as masonry *klinae* (Dunbabin 1991, plus Volpe 2006). In other words, there is no evidence that the *stibadium* was notably less mobile than its predecessor rectangular couches. Indeed, the likely segmented design of wooden *stibadia*, seemingly composed of separate trapezoidal couches

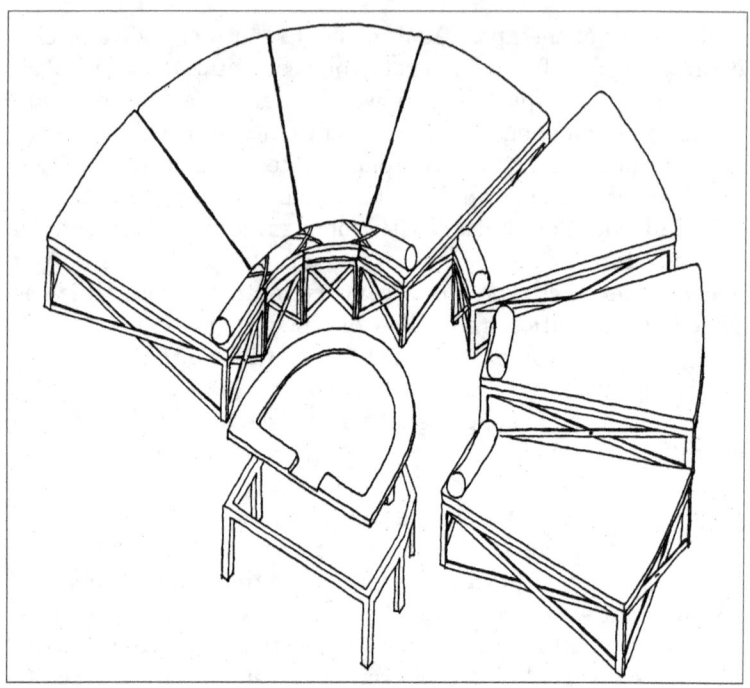

Fig. 18. Reconstruction of a segmented wooden *stibadium* from the Villa of the Falconer, Argos.

laid in a semicircle, suggests particular portability, and even the tables which lay inside the curve of the couch were also likely portable (Åkerström-Hougen 1974, 101-10; Balty 1997, 101, 106; Duval 1984, 464) (Fig. 18).

Furthermore, the notion that dining in an apse was more 'hierarchical' is not immediately obvious from either architecture or seating design. Apsed dining spaces would have had contradictory effects on their viewers and occupants: when viewed from the doorway of the dining room, the apse produces an axial view, culminating at its centre. But it was not typically at the centre that the most important guest lay: while later Roman visual sources depict the principal guest at either one end or at the centre of the couch, the latter in part a product of

2. The Archaeology of Later Roman Houses

taste for symmetrical compositions (Engemann 1982), the textual sources are nearly unanimous in locating the highest ranking guest at the right end of the couch (Mau 1894-, 1205-6; Marquardt and Mau 1886, 1.307-8). In this sense the apse failed to apportion attention along socially hierarchical lines (Volpe 2006, 339). More importantly, and like earlier *triclinia*, apsed halls tended to privilege a view out of the apse towards the decorated floor or the peristyle beyond (cf. Bek 1983, 86-8). The apse thus serves not as a stage, as Ellis claimed, but as a viewing box. The apse also simultaneously forced diners into increased proximity, as the generally more constrained arms of the apse and the measurably narrower *stibadium* would have caused diners to snuggle up with peers and social inferiors alike (Dunbabin 1991, 76). This, along with the generally smaller number of guests one could seat in a single apse versus earlier *triclinia* (Dunbabin 1991, 129-30; Volpe 2006, 338-9), points less towards social hierarchy and more towards social intimacy.

Indeed, the principal prop for the dining 'hierarchization' and 'ritualization' argument derives not from spatial analysis, but from a passage of the Gallic poet and epistolographer Sidonius Apollinaris, who takes elaborate pains to describe the exact seating arrangements, rank of the participants, and stilted conversation at a dinner with the emperor Majorian (*Letters* 1.11.10-17, cited by Ellis 1988, 575; 1997a, 50). But even Sidonius' letter is no straightforward reportage, for the whole passage is a satirical con. Like the Horatian satires it mimics (compare Sidonius, *Letters* 1.11.1 and 1.11.17 with Horace, *Satires* 2.1.82-3 and 2.8.18-95 respectively), its purpose is to expose the vulgarity of the mighty, here the praetorian prefect Paeonius, by highlighting the disparity between the latter's high political rank and his lowly personal qualities. The long *ekphrasis* on the dinner seating (1.11.10) – itself another Horatian borrowing – is a carefully composed symmetry, the odious Paeonius and his equally disparaged companion, Athenius, flanked on either side by men of higher virtue, including, naturally, Sidonius himself (cf. Roberts 1989, 15-22). The emperor Majorian's preference for Sidonius over his ranking rival in the witty repartee that follows demolishes the spatial/social order and exposes the 'real' order – of quality and learnedness – in which Sidonius naturally take precedence. In other words, Sidonius' dinner description is not a description of rank and hierarchy, but a carefully-composed, classically-framed deconstruction of it. To read Sidonius as emblematic of a general social predilection for 'ritualized' or 'hierarchized' behaviour is quite literally to miss the joke.

The notion that the proliferation of the apse necessarily brought with it hierarchy and ritual is, on the basis of both archaeology and a more attentive reading of the textual sources, unconvincing. Yet apses were surely not devoid of social significance. What is perhaps most interesting about the apsed form and its other curved cognates is its unwillingness to be confined to possible reception/dining spaces, where the form might be functionally relevant, and its proliferation into a host of other rooms. At the fifth-century Maison du Cerf at Apamea (Syria) or at the Maison d'Europe at Djemila (see Fig. 17), tiny apsed rooms lay off the peristyle. At Carthage, they commonly formed exedrae off peristyle colonnades (Bullo and Ghedini 2003, 2.112-67). Bi-apsed halls, such as the 50-metre-long example at the fourth(?)-century House of the Governor at Ephesus or the small fourth-century additions to the Maison des Saisons at Sbeitla, display apses capping the ends of long or short passageways (Baldini Lippolis 2002, 196; Bullo and Ghedini 2003, 2.201-3). The phenomenon is probably most visible in rural villas, where lack of spatial constraints allowed late antique builders and their patrons to indulge in extraordinary apsed fantasies. At Carranque in Hispania, apses festoon every corner of the house, from two small rooms off the peristyle, to a bi-apsidal hall, to an exedra facing the main square-in-circle space (Fernández-Galiano ed. 2001) (see Fig. 5); at Cuevas de Soria and Gárgoles (Fig. 19) also both in Hispania, the main room was flanked by tiny hall-like spaces, terminated with tiny apses (Chavarría 2007, 237-40). Piazza Armerina's apses are nearly as impressive as its mosaics – two bi-apsidal halls, semicircular latrines, and a flurry of small

2. The Archaeology of Later Roman Houses

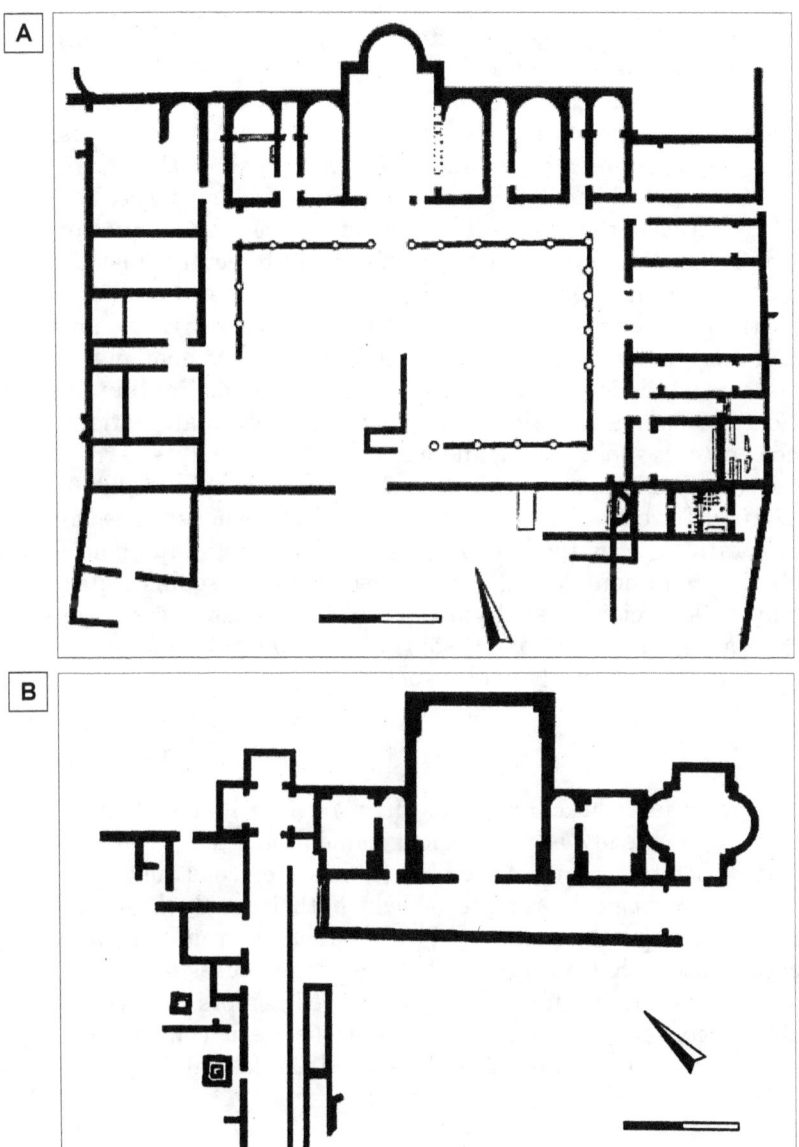

Fig. 19. Villas in Spain. A: Cuevas de Soria; B: Gárgoles.

apsed rooms off the great eastern grouping (Carandini, Ricci and De Vos 1982) (see Fig. 2).

In these instances, it seems highly unlikely that the form is used to accommodate some function. Rather, its form was prized *qua* form, a jewel-like addition to wall surfaces, an intimate spatial pendant to vast courtyards and entrances. The proliferation of the apse in late antique architecture is thus not simply functional or ideological, but, as architectural historians have been at pains to point out, part of the evolution of a particular late antique aesthetic (Schweizer 2005). Strictly formal analysis of Roman domestic architecture has gone out of fashion, but as is clear from Sulpicius Severus and Paulinus of Nola's exchange of building plans and *ekphrases*, late antique homeowners thought long and hard about form and its hermeneutics (Paulinus of Nola, *Letters* 32.9-10, cf. Conybeare 2000, 92-104). To read space as simply a knee-jerk response to social imperatives, as is the current tendency in late antique house studies, is to deny late Roman homeowners the sophisticated and self-conscious visual culture we readily now ascribe to their ancestors (cf. Elsner 1995; Hölscher 2004). The apse and its cognates was surely part of such a culture.

*

In brief, then, the current paradigm on late Roman houses rests on unsteady archaeological foundations. The evidence from which the corpus of such houses has been construed, and the methodological precepts on which their study has proceeded, are both potentially flawed. Just as troubling is a periodization that has assumed late antique houses to be spatially and socially 'different' from their predecessors, and which has in consequence underestimated the deep continuities which are quite as striking as the spatial and formal novelties.

3

Houses and History

The notion of late antique houses as spaces of heightened social stratification and ritualized behaviour was not developed through archaeology alone. Indeed, one of the great breakthroughs ushered in by Ellis and Thébert was their insistence that houses should be read as social machines, products of socio-political circumstances in their respective urban and rural environments. So central is social context to the analysis of these houses that it is often hard to escape the sense that a particular vision of late Roman social relationships has imposed itself on the archaeology. Why the movement through monumentally-punctuated spaces should be 'ritualized' movement, why axiality should imply 'seigneurial' authority, why apsed halls should produce or maintain hierarchies – as noted above, none of these relationships are necessarily obvious from the archaeology. These interpretations are convincing only if one approaches the house with a view of late antique society as hierarchical, ritualized and all the rest. Late antique houses mirror their society because society has, to a certain degree, been read into houses.

It is thus important to understand what model of society lies behind house scholarship, and to shine upon it the light of new work – both archaeological and historical. It is not an easy task; the house paradigm has become so deeply embedded that it is now used to make sense of the very texts which had originally shaped it. One now reads the late Roman agronomist Palladius assuming a 'seigneurial' villa, or the orator Libanius imagining houses populated by his loathed *honorati* (Vera 1999, 291-2; Liebeschuetz 1972, 134, respectively). The paradigm also touches at many points on an evolving social history, one which has become hotly debated in recent years as texts such as the Theodosian Code and the writings of Libanius are subjected to new critical readings. The following thus offers a necessarily abbreviated critique, focused as tightly as possible around the houses themselves.

Patrocinium and houses

All major studies of late Roman houses assume that a nastier, or at least increasingly one-sided, kind of patronage lies behind houses' architectural developments – more and larger reception spaces, separation of reception from dining, or the construction of more impressive rural residences (e.g. Ellis 1988, 575; Thébert 1987, 380, 389-90; Scott 2000, 110; Sfameni 2006b, 186-7; Chavarría 2007, 67-8). The notion of a distinctly late antique brand of patronage is derived from sources like Libanius, who took for granted the total submission of his rural *clientes*, the Christian critic Salvian, who bemoaned that same submission, and the law code edicts that prohibited patrons from offering tax remission in exchange for land and protection (Libanius, *Oration* 47; Salvian, *On the Government of God* 5.8; Theodosian Code 11.24; Codex Justinianus 11.54). When compared with the 'oily, present-giving world' of Cicero, where give-and-take cut across class boundaries and enabled a limited kind of social mobility, later patronage seems a stark thing indeed (MacMullen 1988, 126; Saller 1982). For generations of scholars, late Roman patronage was characterized by a markedly greater social divide between *patronus* and *cliens*, violently coercive capabilities on the part of the patron, and thus the evolution of what had been a quid-pro-quo relationship into something like proto-feudal slavery (Harmand 1955, 205-10; Jones 1964, 775-8; Liebeschuetz 1972, 204-8; Marcone 1998, 362-3; cf. Krause 1987, 1 n. 1).

The recent work of Jens-Uwe Krause and Chris Kelly has described a somewhat different world. Krause's attentive reading of the Theodosian Code and focus on the polemical quality

3. Houses and History

of literary sources such as Salvian and Libanius suggests that late Roman patronage was not substantially different from that of the early empire (Krause 1987; Wickham 2005, 527-9). Clients were not, as a simple reading of these sources might suggest, merely the under-classes, but included senators, *curiales*, rich and poor farmers – the same wide range of people as in the earlier empire. Clients wanted the same thing as their early imperial predecessors – loans, legal help, promotions. Patrons, for their part, never gained any permanent legal control over dependents, nor did patrons' homes seem to have replaced law courts as sites of disputation. Rural patronage remained largely economic in nature, but hardly the Mafia system described by Salvian. Rural patronage actually permitted a certain kind of social mobility as patrons offered alternatives to rural workers looking to change geographic or personal circumstances. Furthermore, as Kelly's work on John Lydus has suggested, money-based alternatives to traditional client-patron relationships developed for men of modest but respectable means. Simple payment in cash for services offered a way out of open-ended personal relationships. New figures – military men, bishops and bureaucrats – now vied with landowners for the loyalties of lesser men, and something like a competitive patronage 'market' grew up, particularly in the countryside (Kelly 2004, 138-85, esp. 170-1; on rural patronage, also Garnsey and Woolf 1989, 162-6). When read in this light, Libanius' treatise on patronage provides a glimpse of a world in which traditional patrons were anything but all powerful – a world that made older senatorial elites, to which Libanius belonged, profoundly uncomfortable (Libanius, *Oration* 47; Harmand 1955, 205-10; Carrié 1976).

In problematizing a particularized 'late antique *patrocinium*', one must also problematize the tacit, but nonetheless problematic implications that have crept into archaeological and art historical assessments. The substantially more powerful *dominus*, so central a figure in even the most cautious house studies, must be reformulated, and the notion of vertiginous social hierarchies lurking behind the attention to and spatial articulation of reception spaces must likewise be reconsidered. The claim, prevalent in villa studies, that the development of super-luxurious provincial villas in the fourth century resulted from harsher relationships between landed patrons and their client *coloni*, must also be rethought.

This is not to argue that markers of social distinction were not part of houses' function, for clearly they were, nor to claim that *domini* did not wield huge power over their dependents. Rather, the new work on patronage suggests that such social distinctions should not be automatically assumed to be more one-sided or more precipitous than in eras past, and that, if anything, the late empire witnessed an expansion of patronage options and alternatives. The apsed audience hall, for instance, rather than being regarded as a venue for the intimidation of *clientes*, might be better understood within a hotly competitive patronage market. It is significant, then, that the cities which have produced houses with large reception spaces rarely produce only one such house, but more frequently, many. It is the multiple, not monopolistic offers of power and influence that may be most significant.

Similarly, images of landlordly power over nature and dependants depicted in mosaic pavements, such as the Great Hunt at Piazza Armerina (see Fig. 3) or the Dominus Julius mosaic from Carthage, are typically interpreted as elaborate structural maps of real social hierarchies in which the *dominus* successfully imparts order, fertility and stasis (e.g. Morand 1994; Schneider 1983). Instead, they might be read, like Libanius' *Oration on Patronage*, as normative rather than positive – idealized images of things as they ought to be in a world where the *dominus*, surrounded by similar competing claims, could not always be assured of successfully ordering his world.

Cities and houses

Ellis' interpretation of the urban *domus* in the East was twined especially tightly around analyses of fourth- to sixth-century urban contexts. In particular, the appearance of great urban

3. Houses and History

houses was tied to the disintegration of participatory municipal government and the concomitant decline of urban civic space. In a model of municipal life formulated by Otto Seek in the early twentieth century and substantially modified by A.H.M. Jones in the 1960s, cities saw their autonomy progressively eroded as the traditional city councillors (*curiales* or *politeuomenoi*), bankrupted by civic duties, were superseded by imperially-appointed outsiders, the *curatores*, or by a narrow band of elites, the *principales* or, in the East, *proteuontes* (Seek 1901, 2.145-90; Jones 1964, 737-63; Liebenam 1897; Petit 1955, 71-91; Leibeschuetz 1972, 167-208; 2001, 37, 111-15; 2006, 470-2). The *principales* particularly play a major role in Ellis' narrative; it is they who are thought to have co-opted municipal government and it is they who are tentatively identified as the owners of great *domus* from North Africa to Asia. As the *fora* and other public spaces of their cities fell into ruin, the *principales* repaired to their homes where in their great reception halls, patronage and 'private' machinations replaced civic life (Ellis 1988, 573-4;1997a, 50; cf. Seek 1901; Jones 1964, 731, 759-61; Kotula 1982; Liebeschuetz 2001, 2-4, 37, 104-36).

The above narrative of the demise of municipal institutions is formulated from two sets of voices – the legal sources that attempt to regulate the relationship between a greatly expanded imperial government and municipal elites, and those, like Libanius, who resented this new relationship because they lost out through its advent. What has emerged from the scholarship of the last two decades are other voices – the town councillors whose prominence diminished but whose jobs continued, the imperial bureaucrats who partnered with them in governing towns, and the tougher, bigger, but nonetheless recognizably Roman style of government that percolates behind the bitter complaints of its critics. These voices do not completely invalidate the narrative that has been used to make sense of late urban *domus*, but they do render it considerably less one-sided. In doing so, they call into question the causal link between the growth of these houses and the decline of municipal institutions.

Houses and Society in the Later Roman Empire

Ever since the advent of the empire, local civic bureaucracies and their treasuries were in tension with imperial honours and a distant court; elevation to equestrian or senatorial status was the siren song that exempted local elites from local duties and pulled their time and money away from their home towns (Italy: Patterson 2006, 185-221; the East: Fernoux 2004, 544-5; in general: Millar 1983, 76-96). Since the second century, these twin enticements had adversely impacted local town finances in Italy. The reports of widespread curial abandonment in the Theodosian Code should thus be understood as part of a very old problem. That this problem would eventually spell the end of *curiales/politeuomenoi* is not in doubt; the timing and overall impact of their demise, however, is more complex than even Jones had appreciated.

Over a third of the Theodosian Code edicts regarding the *curiales* were addressed to the African diocese (Lepelley 1979-81, 243-4); it is their cities where curial abandonment should be most pronounced, and thus it is the hundreds of remodelled North African *domus* which should have housed their oligarchic successors and usurped public government. Claude Lepelley's exhaustive study of the cities of North Africa makes this scenario highly unlikely. As hundreds of inscriptions attest, curial government continued to flourish in North Africa up through the Vandal invasions of the mid-fifth century, and curial rank continued to be a much-desired first step to imperial-level jobs and senatorial status (Lepelley 1979-81, 150-292; Heather 1998, 1988-96, 204-6). As Lepelley has convincingly argued, the angry edicts describe not widespread curial flight, but rather a legalistic attempt to manage the new, multi-stranded relationships between civic offices and a bigger imperial government. Within two generations, Diocletian's (284-305) radical expansion of the imperial bureaucracy and Constantine's (306-337) expansion of the senatorial aristocracy had created a whole host of new career paths that led, eventually, to exemption from civic duties (Heather 1998). The legal chatter sought to ensure that most of these paths continued to lead through, rather than around, local government, grounding

3. Houses and History

the new hierarchies in a prerequisite of local civic service. Their preoccupation with North Africa sounds not the death knell of the class, but its cacophonous life and the imperial government's reliance on curial government to manage that diocese's thousands of cities (Lepelley 1979-81, 243-92; Carrié 2005, 282, 293-4; Heather 1998, 204-6). Thus there is no reason to suppose that the dozens of elite North African houses were owned by a different kind of urban elite, or that their apsed halls had taken over the role of a still-thriving *curia*.

The fifth- to sixth-century cities of the East are a different matter. Even taking into account the general decline of the epigraphic evidence that is our best source for town life, membership in town councils, or *boulai*, from Athens to Antioch crashes in the fourth century while the town councilmen, or *politeuomenoi/bouleutai*, become notably scarce in sources of all kinds (Laniado 2002, 5-9; Liebeschuetz 1972, 174-83; Sironen 1994, 35). Their judicial and euergetistic roles seem to be taken over by other figures, the variously-named *principales, primates, possessores, ktetores, protoi*, or *proteuontes*. The origins of these men are somewhat unclear, but they were probably 'new men' of bureaucratic or military background, rather than the same old *curiales* or local landowners with new titles (cf. Laniado 2002, 177-85; Banaji 2001, 101-70). The function of the various titles is also debated: were these all actual city leaders, or were some titles simply honorary (Liebeschuetz 2001, 104-36)? The title of *principal/proeuton* was not new, but described the 'first men' of the curial order who had acted as a kind of board of directors for large and unwieldy *boulai*, and occupied the top city and provincial positions ever since the first century BC (Seek 1910; Petit 1955, 83 n. 10; Laniado 2002, 204). Their late antique brethren were similarly drawn from the top ranks of urban elites, but by the fifth century this meant non-curial men typically of senatorial rank who were thus exempt from civic duties (Laniado 2002, 133, 161-9, 208). Yet it is precisely in the performance of such duties that we find them, arrayed with the titles that advertise their jobs – organizing grain supply (*sitones*), judging minor court

Houses and Society in the Later Roman Empire

cases (*ekdikos*), or serving as the 'father of their city' (*pater tes poleos*) (Laniado 2002, 214-17; Roueché 1979, 173-85). These were jobs previously managed by the curial order, now seemingly taken up by the 'first men'.

Characterizing these changes to municipal government in terms of a hostile take-over, however, doesn't quite catch the tenor of the transformation, and blaming the *proteuontes* for the 'end of the ancient city' seems to miss the point (Liebeschuetz 2001, 2-4; cf. Whittow 1990; Lavan 2003, 705-10). These 'notables', it is now clear, did not wholly replace the curial order: attentive readings have revealed *politeuomenoi* labouring away at fiscal duties through the seventh century. That is, the notables and the town councillors co-existed, seemingly engaged in different aspects of municipal government with the former clearly on top (Laniado 2002, 1-132; Gascou 1976; DiSegni 1995, 324).

Neither should one wax too nostalgic over *boule* government as forerunners of modern liberal democracies or town councilmen as ardently civic-minded philanthropists. Recent work on Italian and eastern municipal government of the high empire has suggested that many towns were *de facto* run by a narrow clique of families, while in some areas like Syria, these curial elites never regarded the construction and maintenance of their cities as part of their civic office (Italy: Mouritsen 1988; the East: Fernoux 2004; Yon 2002; Sartre-Fauriat 2003; Whittow 1990). By the second century, for all the magnificent spectacle of 600-strong *boulai*, the cities of the Greek East may have born less resemblance to Solon's Athens and more to Tony Soprano's Newark (cf. Liebeschuetz 2001, 121).

The rise of the *proteuontes*, particularly in the fifth and sixth centuries, might better be read as an innovative solution to the age-old tension between town council duties and imperial exemptions. In the *proteuontes*, we find exempt men, increasingly imperial officials who had never held curial office, shouldering civic duties. In some cities, such as Aphrodisias, Caesarea Maritima and Ephesus, they commemorated in poetic verse their construction of new buildings and repair of the old, using

3. Houses and History

their own money as well as that from the city coffers (Aphrodisias and Ephesus: Roueché 1989a, nos 42-4, 89, p. 77; Caesarea: Lehmann and Holum 2000, 58-9). In other words, the *proteuontes* seem to represent an institutionalized effort to fold back into municipal government those men who imperial office and rank had drawn away. It is entirely possible that houses like the so-called Bishop's House at Aphrodisias (see Fig. 13) or the newly-uncovered residences at Caesarea belonged to such 'notables'. But to accuse these houses or their owners of usurping municipal government is to miss the continued workings of such governments, the long dominance such men had had over them, and the urgent need, met by these new ranks and titles, to reintegrate imperial and exempt men into local duties.

The other postulated impresario of urban houses is the imperial bureaucracy. Absconding with a portion of the city's revenue and increasingly intervening in the city's affairs, the bloated bureaucracy of provincial governors is held up as the other culprit in urban decline and the creation of the urban super-*domus* (Ellis 1997a, 50; Liebeschuetz 2001, 110; Jones 1964, 757-9; Palme 1999, 9-100). The rise of the imperial bureaucracy and the shift from *polis* to provincial identity and organization is one of the hallmarks of late imperial politics, and had an enormous impact on urban life (Kelly 2004; Roueché 1998). The expansion of the imperial bureaucracy from a few thousand in the second century to some 30,000 by the sixth century placed imperial servants on the ground in far larger numbers (Kelly 2004, 111). The multiplication of provinces and the fiscal emphasis on the provincial unit focused economic activity in provincial capitals, often to the detriment of other cities (Liebeschuetz 2001, 37-9; Roueché 1989b; Ward-Perkins 1998; Lavan 2001a). Many of the cities that boast large numbers of late Roman houses were, at the time those houses were built, provincial and/or diocesan capitals – Athens, Aphrodisias, Caesarea, Apamea – and it is reasonable to suppose that many housed the upper echelons of provincial government.

Again, to connect the appearance of such houses with the cessation of municipal politics at the hands of imperial officials is probably off the mark. The extraordinary expansion of imperial government did not take the place of municipal institutions, but partnered with them (Lepelley 1979-81, 243-92; Carrié 2005; cf. Liebeschuetz 2001, 121). Officials like the *curator rei publicae*, previously an imperially-appointed watchdog over municipal treasuries, was, by the late empire, folded into the local *curia*, a local man nominated by his peers and approved by the governor to act as chief civic magistrate (Lepelley 1979-81, 168-90; Burton 1979). Likewise, at least in the Roman West, the *curia* remained the seedbed of talent from which the imperial bureaucracy drew its recruits: the 70 or so imperial *officiales* included among an early fourth-century list of local grandees at Timgad have been plausibly identified as coming from local curial families (Carrié 2005, 281; Kelly 2004, 146-8), and the many laws forcing *curiales* to complete their municipal *munera* before aspiring to imperial jobs make it clear that the main path from town to imperial government lay through the *curia* (Lepelley 1979-81, 243-39; Heather 1998, 196). The emperor's men were thus often local men and the expanding imperial government offered expanded opportunities to up-and-coming hometown boys (Lavan 2001a).

Rather than top-down oppression by a narrow elite, the enlarged imperial bureaucracy brought with it a bottom-up expansion of social opportunity (MacMullen 1964, 50; Hopkins 1965). Behind the rise of provincial governors was the rise of a huge bureaucratic class – lawyers, paralegals, clerks, scribes and notaries (Palme 1999). These were positions which required decent Latin and thus the education which only curial-type wealth could buy. Their modest pay could be augmented by the newly-established administrative fees and the possibility of advancement (Kelly 2004, 26-36). Indeed, Jairus Banaji has suggested that these persons' gold-based salaries ushered in a social revolution in the fifth- and sixth-century East, as bureaucrats and military men elbowed their way into the traditional landholding elite and eventually displaced them

3. Houses and History

(Banaji 2001, 101-70). The rash of new farms, small and large, that appear in the hinterlands of many eastern cities from Greece to Palestine during the fourth and fifth centuries may be the remnants of this new 'gold' class (e.g. Vanhaverbeke and Waelkens 2003, 241-84; Lewin and Pellegrini 2006; Banaji 2001). The provincial capitals, with their hundreds-strong *officia*, would have bustled with these up-and-comers, while local lads of respectable but unprepossessing families would have been drawn there like moths to a flame.

Again, if we want to relate these developments to houses, it is the multiplicity of fine *domus* and the range of wealth, from the modestly renovated Hanghäuser to the huge Theatre House in cities like Ephesus (see Figs 11, 12, 14, 15), which should strike us most. These houses, like the data from the rural field surveys, seem to bespeak an expanded, heterogeneous elite, connected in some way with this expanded imperial bureaucracy. Rather than the rise of a narrow clique of grandees, the range of house size and appointments parallels the broadening base of imperial bureaucracy that pulled everyone from ex-itinerant labourers to 'old money' into its orbit.

Finally, the model that posits the rise of the elite super-*domus* at the expense of civic government points to a decay in civic infrastructure. *Fora* were blanketed by shops, town halls and other buildings of government fallen into ruin – the disintegration of urban fabric is said to document the collapse of municipal government as the *principales* governed from behind the closed doors of their homes.

Most cities eventually experienced the above-described changes, but a surge of new work on late antique urbanism now permits us to be increasingly precise as to their nature and timing (e.g. Lavan 2001b; Liebeschuetz 2001). It is becoming clear that, as a general rule, cities that saw significant *domus* construction did not experience major infrastructure decline at the time the *domus* were built. Space does not permit an extended analysis, and city or region-based analysis of epigraphic and legal evidence alongside house archaeology remains a major *desideratum* for future research. A quick sampling of cities with notable numbers of elite *domus*, however, reveals some interesting trends.

Bulla Regia, a modest Hadrianic colony in Africa Proconsularis, has been only partially excavated, but some sixteen houses occupied and mostly refurbished in the late fourth/early fifth century, including two with alleged near-door reception and dining spaces, were found among its remains (Beschaouch, Hanoune and Thébert 1977; Bullo and Ghedini 2003, 2.33-72) (see Fig. 8). At this time, judging from the city's admittedly limited epigraphic corpus, the city had an active curial order, headed by a *curator rei publicae*, while the provincial proconsul, based in Carthage, as well the city's exempt *clarissimi*, also took an active interest in the town's maintenance. The city archives had been recently rebuilt as well as other public buildings and one or two sets of new public baths, while Augustine complained about the city's active theatre (Lepelley 1979-81, 2.87-90; Thébert 2003, 133-5).

At Djemila, ancient Cuicul, in Numidia, some six houses seem to have been renovated during the later fourth century, while the Maison de Bacchus was expanded in the early fifth century (Blanchard-Lemée 1975; Baldini Lippolis 2002, 189-94; Lepelley 1979-81, 2.402-15) (see Fig. 17). In this period, the urban fabric had been renewed, with new or restored porticoes, baths, judicial basilicas, and market. By the late fourth century, many of these works, and control of the city government, lay in the hands of three great families, the Rutilii, the Pomponii and the Tullii. They did so while serving in the top jobs of the decurial order, particularly the perpetual civic priesthood, working alongside an active *curia* (Lepelley 1979-81, 414).

Ostia, port city of Rome, has produced over a dozen late antique houses, most carved out of the bottom floors of apartment houses, and most dating to the late third or early fourth century, with constant later renovations (Becatti 1948; Pavolini 1986; Tione 1999). This expansion of elite quarters, seeming abandonment of some apartments, the degradation of some parts of the city, particularly shops, and ascension of nearby Portus to municipal status, all led Pavolini to suggest

3. Houses and History

that the city had lost its commercial character and had become a bedroom community for Rome or Portus' senatorial class (Pavolini 1986, 251-2, 268-76). Yet the external staircases of some *domus* suggest that the upper-storey apartments continued to function, as did many of their attendant shops. The urban centre along the main roads was renovated, including the forum baths, the theatre, the public latrines and a series of fountains and fountain houses, while a flurry of honorific statues describe a populace hungry for attention (Pavolini 1986 252-2; 268-76; Meiggs 1960, 92-7; Gering 2004). The impresario was often the *praefectus annonae*, chief of the grain supply, who, despite the ascent of Portus, his nominal seat, seems to have served as both patron and *curator* in Ostia (Meiggs 1960, 96). As Pavolini noted, the modest size and appointments of the Ostian *domus* are hard to tie to the occasional epigraphic references to great Roman senatorial families like the Volusiani and the Anicii (Pavolini 1986, 276). It is the *praefectus annonae* and his small army of mid-level bureaucrats whose presence appears most boldly in the city's new civic building projects and who are the most likely homeowners.

Moving East brings different house and urban chronologies and altered urban institutions. After a series of raids, late fourth/early fifth century Athens, capital of the province of Achaia, was bustling with repairs. On the Areopagus and in the Agora new houses were going up in multiples, some of which seem to have been rebuilt after the Gothic sack of 395 (Frantz 1988; Castrén 1994; Baldini Lippolis 2002, 147-58). While the *boule* seems to have shrunk to some 300 members, it and the urban *demes* continued to give out honours. The provincial proconsul and the archons took the lead in building and repairs, while sophists and philosophers ornamented the city with statues dedicated to imperial officials (Sironen 1994).

At Aphrodisias, provincial capital of Caria in Asia Minor, the great urban *domus* find their richest phase somewhat later, in the fifth century (Roueché 1989a, xxv, 35-122; Ratté 2001; Berenfeld 2002; Baldini Lippolis 2002, 119-22). The urban fabric was in generally good shape; the construction of the great public peristyle, restorations of the civil basilica, and the conversion of the stadium into an amphitheatre had all been arranged in the fourth and early fifth century by the resident provincial governors and their *princeps officii*. Beginning in the mid-fifth century, individual donors reappear, some of whom, like one Ampelius, are named as *pater tes polios* (father of the city), and undertake the further restoration of the agora, new fountains and the refurbishment of the council house, now a place for spectacles. Councilmen persist until at least the fifth or sixth century when they are found acting as a provincial, rather than *polis* group, honouring the praetorian prefect of the East (Roueché 1989a, no. 36).

At Ephesus, the earthquakes of the late fourth century wreaked havoc on the diocesan capital; in their wake, a range of elite houses was either rebuilt or modestly refurbished, from the huge Theatre House and the so-called Governor's Palace of uncertain date, to the more modest renovations in Hanghaus I (Lang-Auinger 1996, 204-6; Miltner 1956; 1959). Great efforts were made to restore the urban infrastructure, although some areas remained in ruin or given over to private construction (Foss 1979; Scherrer 1995; Thür 1996) (Fig. 20). Much of this work was undertaken by the proconsul of Asia, while private donors undertook some smaller, but prominent projects – new baths were donated by the woman Scholastica, while other private donors built fountains and nymphea. By the mid-fifth century, provincial government was aided by the *pater tes polios*, which at Ephesus may have been a jointly-held rank (Roueché 1989a, 77).

These very different house/city stories illustrate the range of urban environments in which *domus* refurbishments took place. Some trends, however, may transcend individual histories. The decline of civic infrastructure impacted all cities eventually, but as is now clear, local circumstances varied enormously. While basilicas and temples were less often maintained (as they had been since the late second century), restored or newly-constructed baths, colonnaded streets, shopping areas and entertainment facilities were the centres of an

3. Houses and History

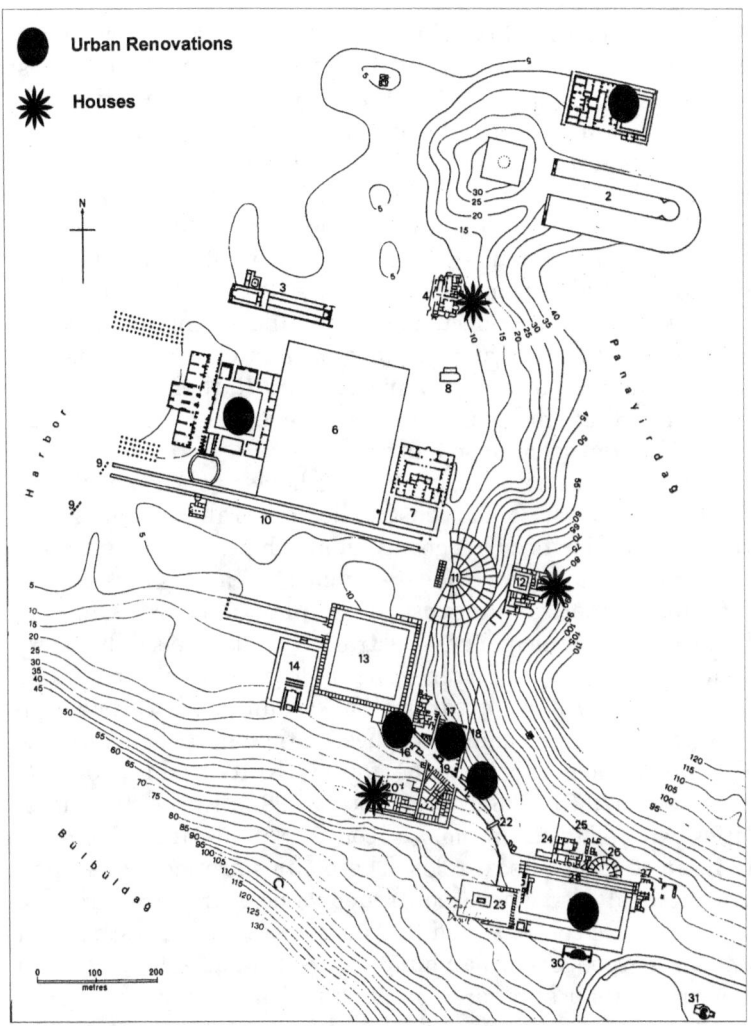

Fig. 20. Ephesus, city plan showing late antique houses and late antique urban improvements.

'urbanism of sociability' which, in those cities that saw significant house construction, continued to chug along in a modest way (cf. Patterson 2006, 90-183). Thus, in those cities that boasted a number of elite homes, urban infrastructure was typically maintained at the time the houses in question were constructed. There are obvious exceptions to this pattern – Luni in Italy, with its two fine houses and crumbling forum, being the most famous – but the overall trend seems quite the opposite (Ward-Perkins 1978; Zaccaria Ruggiu 1991, 103-4). In other words, the well-documented and increasingly well-dated decline of civic urbanism cannot be related to monumental *domus* building in any convincing way. Rather, moments of house building and moments of civic investment, even though small in scale, seem to go hand-in-hand.

The potential impresarios of these homes vary from West to East. In the West *domus* construction generally coincides with the continuation of curial government. This is particularly true in North Africa, where evidence for curial health is particularly plentiful. Imperial bureaucrats also play major roles in both building and municipal administration. Thus, especially in provincial capitals, a heterogeneous mixture of provincial *officiales, clarissimi* of various backgrounds, as well as *curiales,* would have comprised these cities' elite homeowners. *Principales* are rarely to be found (Kulikowski 2004, 43; Lepelley 1979-81, 233, *contra* Kotula 1982). In the East, most cities with significant *domus* concentrations find the *boule* reduced to minor fiscal roles. These cities are most often provincial capitals, where continued civic infrastructure and building were concentrated (Lavan 2001a). Urban government and a resurgence of urban building are organized by provincial governors, their staff, and, by the mid-fifth century, the newly institutionalized *principales,* who seem to work in concert with imperial officials and the remnants of civic government. Other private donors – from philosophers to exempt *illustres* – reappear after two centuries of quietude. The potential impresarios of eastern *domus* are thus a different, but a no less heterogeneous group than their somewhat earlier western brethren.

3. *Houses and History*

The countryside and houses

The study of late Roman villas in the West has proceeded from a more attentive study of local context than has that of urban houses, and in general has paid careful attention to recent work in both landscape archaeology and rural social history (e.g. Chavarría 2007; Sfameni 2006b; Balmelle 2001). Although most provincial villas exhibit somewhat different spatial qualities than do urban houses – individual spaces are often far larger, they devote far more space to entrance courtyards and they often exhibit more coherent, totalizing rebuilding phases – the general conclusions derived from Thébert and Ellis' spatial analyses – privatization and hierarchization – are regularly repeated in villa scholarship (Sfameni 2006b, 178-9; Scott 2000, 108; 2004, 52; cf. Mulvin 2002, 41; Chavarría 2007, 94 are more cautious). The notable expansion and elaboration of rural villas in the fourth century (with some continuation in the early fifth) in certain areas of the Roman West is thus frequently understood as a product of a newly hierarchical countryside, a notion which is also widely repeated in the historical literature (e.g. Garnsey and Whittaker 1998, 322; Whittaker and Garnsey 1998, 299-310).

In many villa studies, the notion of a significantly larger estate plays a major explanatory role, making sense of what in certain provinces (Britain, Aquitaine, Hispania, Pannonia and perhaps southern Italy) seem to be the largest, and certainly the most luxurious, phases of Roman villa architecture. The notion that estates were bigger, and more land was owned by fewer people, is axiomatic in late Roman economic studies. While appreciation of the fragmented, parcelled nature of Roman land holding has grown, it is consistently assumed that in late antiquity, these dispersed pieces amounted to significantly bigger estates, owned by fewer people (Jones 1964, 773; Vera 1995, 331; 2001, 628; cf. Sarris 2004 on the East). Larger estates produce bigger, grander villa residences, while the concentration of land in the hands of the few produces more precipitous social hierarchies (Sodini 1995, 153; Chavarría

2007, 53-4; Sfameni 2006b, 175-6; Scott 2000, 54; Vera 1994, 136-8).

It is important to note on what fragile grounds such assumptions rest, particularly in the western provinces of the fourth and early fifth centuries – that is, the areas where fine rural villas are thickest on the ground. While it is clear that the properties of fourth-century landowners were highly fragmented, their portfolios in some cases reaching across several provinces, it is far less clear that the average size of localized holdings was necessarily larger. The most often cited anecdotal evidence – Melania the Younger's annual income or Ausonius' brief description of his estate – are poor spokesmen; the former is an advertisement for radical Christian mega-charity; the later a meditation on the self, using a poetics enamoured of enumeration (*Life of Melania the Younger* [ed. Gorce] 15, 19; Palladius, *Lausiac History* 61; Ausonius, *Domestica* 1.17-28; Roberts 1989, 41-3; 55, 59). As has been amply demonstrated for the high empire, literary statements about the size of rural estates reveal little or nothing about actual real estate, but are more often vehicles for social criticism (Martin 1995). In any case, these texts are snapshots and cannot be readily compared with anything before or after. The thin epigraphic evidence – principally the Ligures Baebiani, Veleia and Lamasba tablets of the second and early third centuries, and the Magnesia, Hermopolis and Volcei registers from the fourth, are difficult to compare – they measure different things (land, tax, productive capacity) and they hail from different regions. If they are laid together, they show a relatively consistent concentration of land in the hands of a few families, but they fail to show any clear trend towards greater concentration (Duncan-Jones 1990, 129-42; Vera 1991, 467-9).

Field survey is often used to argue for larger estates, citing either a decreased number of small sites as evidence of increased concentration of properties, or the appearance of such small sites as evidence for the farms of tenant *coloni* and the decline of small landowners (e.g. larger estates: Vera 1995, 331-4; Cambi et al. 1994; Patterson 2006, 57-8; continuity of

3. Houses and History

smaller estates: Lewit 1991, 30-3). The same interpretations of contrary data yield a cautionary tale: 'You can dig up a villa but you cannot dig up its land tenure' (Stevens 1966, 108). C.T. Steven's much cited axiom is no less true today, and thus far field survey has not been made to yield any information about estate size, organization or ownership patterns. Finally, and perhaps most importantly, there is virtually no diachronic evidence, indeed, almost no evidence at all, for estate size in those provinces where late, luxury villas are thickest on the ground – Hispania, Aquitaine, south-west Britain and perhaps Pannonia (Vera 1997, 186, 199; Banaji 2001, 171-2; cf. Gorges 1979; Black 1987, 55-69). In short, the evidence for bigger estates or for greater concentration of land in the fourth-century West is shakier than has perhaps been appreciated.

Similar problems confront the most convincing paradigm for estate management. Domenico Vera has argued that the third century saw a marked shift in the way estates were managed; by the third century, more focused, slave-based agriculture gave way to dispersed holdings let to tenants. Rent collection, rather than the sale of agricultural produce, became the predominant source of income for elites who now spent more time on their estates, monitoring their investment. Late Roman villas were the result – luxurious rural homes for 'in-residence' landowners (Vera 1994; 2001). Vera's nuanced and sophisticated model is based on an evolution from slave to tenant-based agriculture, thus explaining why late antique villas look 'different': while late republican/early imperial villas like the Tuscan Settefinestre included both elite residence and workers quarters, the later villas were permanent, luxury residences of elites while workers and tenants were housed elsewhere (see also Carandini, Ricci and De Vos 1982). This is not the place to rehearse the arguments for or against the predominance of slave agriculture in the late republic and early empire, except to note that the issue is controversial and both the textual and archaeological evidence are hotly contested (cf. Carandini 1985; 1989; Giardina and Schiavone 1981, versus Capogrossi Colognesi 1986; Neeve 1984; Marzano 2007,

125-53). What is important is that the model probably only applies to Italy (Kehoe 2007, 553-6) – which, interestingly, has thus far yielded a relatively smaller cache (about 30) of late luxury villas (see Sfameni 2006b). There is very little evidence for major slave-based holdings in the provinces, certainly not in those which interest us here, where it is generally accepted that tenancy or free labour had always been the norm (Wickham 2005, 264). Overall, then, a major transformation in land holding in the western provinces between the first and fourth centuries seems hard to sustain (cf. Wickham 2005, 264-80). The explosion of luxury villas in these places, therefore, cannot be attributed to major changes in land tenure in any clear or obvious way.

Finally, there is the matter of rural hierarchies. The principal social relationship lurking behind most, although not all, villa studies is that between *dominus* and *colonus* (e.g. Scott 2000, 106-7; Sfameni 2006b, 184-7). The great entrance courts and the mosaic-covered audience halls are thought to be a product of rural dominance, even if the dusty *colonus*, cap in hand, never made it past the main door. The image of the all-powerful late antique *dominus* is an old one – propagated by Romans themselves on their mosaic floors, and disparaged in sources like Salvian's deprecations (Salvian, *On the Government of God*, 4.4-6, 5.7-8). It depends in large part on a complementary negative image – that of the downwardly mobile *colonus*. This image has recently been given a thorough, if controversial, cleaning (summarized in Wickham 2005, 520-5). The Theodosian Code seems to describe the progressive bondage of *coloni* to the land and their progressive decline from free farmer to something resembling a slave (Theodosian Code 5.17.1; 5.18; 5.19; Codex Justinianus 11.51.1; 11.48.21; Rostovtzeff 1910; Jones 1964, 795-812). Such a reading of the Code, it has emerged, is misleading. As Jean-Michele Carrié has argued, the Code is not concerned with the social status of *coloni*, or the private contractual relationships between *dominus* and *colonus*. Ultimately, the Code is not concerned with *dominus/colonus* relationships at all, but with tax, and tying tax respon-

3. Houses and History

sibility to places (and thus people) on the ground (Carrié 1982; 1983; 1997; Grey 2007). Jairus Banaji has alternatively suggested that this fiscal *adscriptio* was itself simply the fiscalization of 'free' labour relationships which had existed in private contracts for centuries (Banaji 1997; cf. Mirkovic 1997). Furthermore, both the Code and the papyrological evidence hint at something more complex than a unidirectional *dominus/ colonus* relationship. Tenants might and did protest against their landlords – when foisted with a new owner, unfair tax obligations, or a rapacious bishop (e.g. *Life of Melania the Younger* [ed. Gorce], 10; Augustine, *Letters* 20*.10). The laws that tied tenants to their land for fiscal reasons also forbade landlords from raising their rent or forcibly removing them (Codex Justinianus 11.50.1-2 (325-6); 11.48.7 (371)). The seemingly inconsistent edicts on *coloni* and diverse use of the term 'colonus' betray a huge variety of private contractual relationships between landlord and tenant, many of which were probably matters of long-standing local tradition, around which the law was forced to work (Grey 2007; Wickham 2005, 523-4). The evidence for such written contracts, and for litigious *coloni*, is significant, hinting at an often literate, legally-savvy group (Vera 1997, 206-9). In short, the generalized portrait of *dominus/colonus* relationships has become far more complex, while a particularized 'late antique' colonate, at least as a social position, is now in real doubt.

Many of the recent villa studies have taken note of this work, but its implications have perhaps not been fully realized. Again, the first issue is periodization; if the novelty of the Theodosian Code lies not in the status or treatment of tenants, but new tax systems designed to assure land-based tax revenue, then the 'newness' of *dominus/colonus* relationships, and thus a real change in tenants' social status, is harder to pin down. There is no doubt that poor tenant farmers of the fourth and fifth centuries were miserable – but were they significantly more miserable than in the second century? (cf. Scheidel 2000; Wickham 2005, 524). This is less clear, particularly since scholars cannot agree that their tax burdens were, in fact, higher (cf.

Bowman 1980; Bagnall 1985; Krause 1987, 311; versus Jones 1959; 1964, 468-9; Wickham 2005, 62-6). In short, complicating the portrait of the powerless tenant suggests that the relationship between landowner and tenant was not only, or even most productively, comprehensible as a one-way power relationship or a set of social binaries.

The notion that the fourth-century 'villa-boom' is tied to new, more hierarchical, more oppressive rural relationships should thus be posed as a question, not as a given. The basic props of this argument – the increasing size of estates, a major change in tenurial relationships, the marked widening of the social gulf between landowner and tenants – are highly tenuous, particularly for the western regions of the empire where monumental later Roman villas are thickest on the ground. As regards all these matters, in these regions we have very little evidence at our disposal. What evidence we do have – mostly the secondary testimony of field survey – bespeaks no radical changes from the second to the fourth/early fifth century, but rather continuity of the same types of settlement patterns to the mid-fifth or even sixth century. Such evidence provides no indication of tenurial patterns; it does, however, suggest that a substantially 'different' late antique villa system is probably a chimera.

*

As this brief overview has suggested, the historical model of social relationships which has so influenced the study of later Roman houses is largely out of date. Based upon precepts set out in the previous century, it has been superseded, or provided with more nuance, in the work of the last two decades. The emphasis on hierarchization that so characterized earlier models has been shown to be overstated, a product of periodized assumptions about late antiquity as a proto-Middle Ages. In its place, new histories do not deny the maintenance of stark social distinctions, but draw attention to the long history such distinctions had in Roman social relationships. These histories

3. Houses and History

suggest that what is new about late antique social relationships is often their rhetorical garb, rather than any qualitative escalation in hierarchies. Many of these studies have likewise emphasized the new venues of social competition that emerged in the late empire. Like the archaeological evidence, these new social histories fail to support the notion of the house as an increasingly blunt instrument of social control or a manifestation of a hierarchical society run by a narrow oligarchy. Instead, they stress the continuity with earlier social relationships and the possibility that houses continued to serve as loci of social competition.

4

New Directions

The preceding critique of late antique house paradigms suggests a number of cautionary tales – about the tacit persistence of medieval-oriented architectural teleologies, and about *a priori* periodization that has often dictated the results of spatial and social analysis. Above all, however, it suggests a more complex relationship between houses and society than has been the norm.

Houses and 'society'

It is tempting to use domestic space to reconstitute social hierarchies, and to tie social-historical change to concomitant changes in the form of houses. Even Bourdieu, whose Berber house analysis cried out against a reading of social rules from architectural form, ended by treating houses as 'objectified history' (Bourdieu 1977, 79, critiqued by King 2000). But houses are not mirrors, or at least not very clear ones, and they reflect society only through a dark glass (Grahame 2000, 2-3). For one, houses and 'society' exist in a constant tug-of-war: houses are imbued with a blueprint for social relationships by their designers; inhabitants push back against those blueprints, reinterpreting and reshaping them through the very act of inhabiting (Smith and Bugni 2006; Gieryn 2002). Artifact analysis reveals this tussle, finding in pots and lamps and furniture fittings a constant reconfiguration of domestic space by the people who inhabited it.

Likewise, we tend to interpret the elite houses of late antiquity as anthropologists have treated so-called 'vernacular' architecture – knee-jerk, largely unconscious building acts to meet the most basic socio-economic needs and to symbolize social values (cf. Rapoport 1969; Bourdieu 1977; cf. Geertz 1983). Yet all houses, and elite houses particularly, are also intentional forms, a product of design in which the object, as itself, communicates social values. That is, the spaces of these houses do not simply act as stages for action, but are deliberately crafted for consumption *qua* forms (Gieryn 2002, 42-3). In other words, design matters. The apse is a good example: its use in dining/reception spaces is functional, while in hallways, mini-chambers and *exedrae* it is deployed as itself, a piece of architectural virtuosity. In short, houses reflect society as poetry does – through the distorting lenses of subversion and style – and it is on those terms that we must be prepared to consider them.

Houses and history

The difficulty of that project should not deter us from using houses to study social history, for there is much about late antique houses which remains food for careful social-historical thought. This is not the place to offer a new paradigm in place of the old; however, three brief observations about the house corpus might point the way towards future research and suggest some reasons why late antique houses might have been particularly potent instruments of manipulative rhetoric.

The first regards periodization. Most of the scholarship on late antique houses has proceeded from the assumption that late antique houses must be spatially and socially distinct from earlier Roman houses. It is assumed that they must be representative of their distinct period – late antiquity – and its special qualities as a bridge between ancient and medieval worlds. We have seen how misleading many of these assumptions have been, and have argued that most of the 'distinctiveness' of later Roman houses is not very distinctive at all. Increased 'privacy', hierarchy, ritualization, functional and hierarchical distinction of space most often turn out to be the

4. New Directions

result of a simplistic application of a particular social historical model onto domestic architecture. On the contrary, we have suggested that many of the allegedly 'unique' qualities of late antique houses are actually shared with earlier houses from their respective regions – a variety of enclosed and permeable sorts of domestic spaces; a continued reference to and interaction with their respective urban landscapes; the multifunctionality of almost all domestic spaces; and above all, their use and manipulation as agents of social competition. In short, late Roman houses are Roman houses, and cannot be properly understood while fenced off by the periodizing boundaries of 'late antiquity'.

This does not mean, however, that later Roman houses cannot, or should not be historically contextualized, or that fourth- to sixth-century social context doesn't have something to tell us about houses' meaning and function. Instead of proceeding from an assumption of difference, or an *a priori* set of ideas about late antique society, an alternative study of late antique houses ought to begin from the houses themselves. One place to start may be the very basic issue of chronology. As discussed above, the corpus of later Roman houses is still badly dated. However, even assuming that careful excavation might shift many dates by as much as a half-century, the corpus displays a certain, even remarkable periodicity. The fourth century seems to see a massive surge in elite house construction, remodelling and redecoration, focused perhaps in the century's second half (Ellis 2007, 11). In the cities of the East, the early to mid-fifth century sees another, more modest spike, while the first half of the sixth century sees still less. The fourth-century surge particularly begs the question why. If, as suggested above, we cannot assume that houses are a simple 'reflection' of social or economic trends, the question must be, 'Why did fourth-century elites, of all levels, choose to invest in their houses, and what did those elites expect houses to do?'

The seeds of one answer have been kicking around in house scholarship for a decade, namely the Constantinian reform of the senatorial aristocracy, in which Constantine and his successors greatly expanded the number of senators, and number of career paths that led to senatorial status (Heather 1998). Some scholars have seen in the expansion of the senatorial order a concomitant expansion in senatorial-style *domus*: more senators, more fine houses, or with more nuance, the houses represent the 'self-display' of a bigger, self-conscious group (Sfemani 2006b, 182-9; Guidobaldi 1986, 227-8; Chavarría 2007, 112-13; generally Salzman 2002, 43-9).

This interpretation, while certainly correct in one respect, may miss more important and complicated implications. As new work has suggested, it is important to view Constantine and his successors' expansion of the senatorial order as a necessary sequel to Diocletian's fiscal and economic reforms of the previous decades (Lepelley 1986). Diocletian's massive expansion of the military and the bureaucracy required similarly massive recruitment for military and bureaucratic personnel. For the most part (and contrary to earlier speculation), the old senatorial elites continued to monopolize the highest positions (Jacques 1986). Other jobs, particularly those in the military and provincial *officia*, drew on other sources of talent – army brats and lower-level town councilmen. Diocletian elevated these offices to the knighthood, or equestrian status, and the equestrian order expanded as a consequence. The goal was not to privilege a bourgeois class of mid-level elites, as Rostovzteff once thought: rather, as Claude Lepelley has shown, the purpose was to provide a title synonymous with old-style Roman *dignitas* – the knighthood – for a new kind of bureaucracy (Lepelley 1986, 231).

The consequence, however, was not exactly what Diocletian had intended: equestrian parvenus accumulated considerable political and military power, but real wealth, not to mention old-school civic status, still rested in the same senatorial and municipal hands. The Constantinian expansion of the senatorial order sought to solve the consequent social dissonance (Heather 1998, 184-9; Hopkins 1965). By using the single gold standard of senatorial status as the pinnacle for bureaucratic and military careers, Constantine and his successors sought to

4. New Directions

unite very different paths for advancement by dangling at their apex the most coveted traditional honour – the senatorial robe. What is potentially significant about the Constantinian reforms is not so much that there were suddenly more people who required nice houses; non-senatorial knights and local town councilmen were not so different in wealth and status than newly-minted, low-level provincial senators (Lepelley 1986, 231-2). Rather, Constantine's reforms were a response to a suddenly heterogeneous aristocracy, or better, a now bewildering variety of aristocracies, all of which were highly competitive in nature and which themselves produced competition between cities and the imperial service for the best men (Heather 1998, 205; Millar 1983, 96). The reforms in turn ushered in a scramble for senatorial rank and its attendant exemptions through the diverse available channels (Heather 1998, 188-92), while the increasingly numerous senators created an internal pecking-order, seeking to distinguish old money from new, super-rich from moderately prosperous. In short, the Diocletianic and Constantinian rank reforms produced not simply more elites, but more heterogeneous, more competitive elites.

The traditional locus of elite competition and distinction in the Roman world was the home. Thus, the precipitous investment in domestic architecture, an architecture which employed a sophisticated, civic-oriented aesthetic, may be located within a half-century-long climax of rank reform and its competitive manipulation by elites and elite-wannabes. In other words, from a purely social-historical perspective, it is the competition between newly heterogeneous and competitive elites, not the domination of those elites over inferiors, which marks the house-boom era of the fourth to early fifth centuries.

Houses and geography

The second avenue of approach, which must be reconciled with historical context, is indicated by geography. Thanks to the careful cataloguing work of the past decade and to the now-significant numbers of late antique houses known from excavation, the geographic distribution of such houses is coming into focus. Contrary to assumption, late antique houses with major architectural modifications do not appear everywhere. Even taking into account regional disparities in research, elite houses seem to appear in clusters, be it in urban or rural areas. Urban houses tend to aggregate in provincial and diocesan capitals, such as Rome and Constantinople, Aphrodisias, Athens, Ephesus, Sardis, Mérida, Milan, Trier, or other places where imperial administrators were thick on the ground, like Ostia. North Africa looks to be an exception with concentrations of elite houses in cities without these types of status. This is not to suggest that all such capitals or administration points have produced houses; it is merely to point to a possible correlation between concentrations of houses and points of imperial administration. Similarly, monumental rural villas seem to cluster in five or six regions: in three areas of south-western Britain, in Aquitaine, in western and northern Hispania, in parts of Pannonia, and perhaps around Trier and in southern Italy/Sicily (Scott 2000; Sodini 1997, 519).

This spotty rather than uniform geography suggests that the need to invest in house building was not a general social imperative. Rather, it was a choice made locally, to do locally-advantageous social work. This seems to run counter to the social-historical background of the Constantinian reforms, for surely such social changes would be felt everywhere equally. Closer examination of these 'house-hotspots' should thus reveal something of the more particular social logic which allowed them to function.

Most of the urban house-hotspots were administrative centres, and the great majority were provincial capitals. Administrative centres had always attracted elites, but after the social reforms of the early fourth century, the origins and career patterns of those elites would have become particularly diverse. Provincial and diocesan capitals were the places where the old and new paths to social advancement met (Lavan 2001a). They were the seat of the provincial governor or dioce-

4. New Directions

san vicar with his small army of bureaucrats. They were the sometimes-headquarters for the pan-provincial generals and hosted an increasingly city-billeted army. And they remained important as themselves – as local cities, dominated by a governing municipal elite whose own order, which might range from ex-itinerant labourers to senators' sons, was highly diverse (Lepelley 1979-81, 318-25; Carrié 2005, 306). In most regions, provincial capitals gradually became the sole venue for administrative activity and thus singular points of attractions for these elites, while other cities sank into obscurity. The exception of North Africa, with its spread of fine houses outside provincial capitals, may be due to the particular expansion and dispersal of these three kinds of elites – bureaucrat, military and curial – into towns without capital status and to the particular vibrancy of town councils in that region (Kelly 2004, 147; LeBohec 2007; 2005, 211-12; Lepelley 1979-81, 150-292). In short, then, cities that have concentrations of houses saw not just an expanded number of senators, but a concentrated mixture of diverse kinds of elites. It was these two factors – concentration, as provincial capitals gradually claimed a monopoly over all administrative functions to the exclusion of other kinds of cities, and diversity, as the various kinds of elites multiplied – which made these cities intense competitive arenas. This is the likely local social-political background behind the rise of multiple fine *domus* in these particular centres.

Rural life leaves fewer traces for the social historian and the background of regional villa hotspots is not yet so clear, but some hypotheses suggest themselves (Fig. 21). All the possible regions with notable monumental villa concentrations – Pannonia, Aquitaine, Hispania, south-west Britain and southern Italy/Sicily – had relatively low concentrations of active urban centres. And yet, as new research is suggesting, each of these rural regions may have had particular concentrations of imperial administrative presence, either through a focused taxation apparatus or through the military.

In Pannonia, later Roman monumental villas abandon the suburban topography of the early empire and instead appear

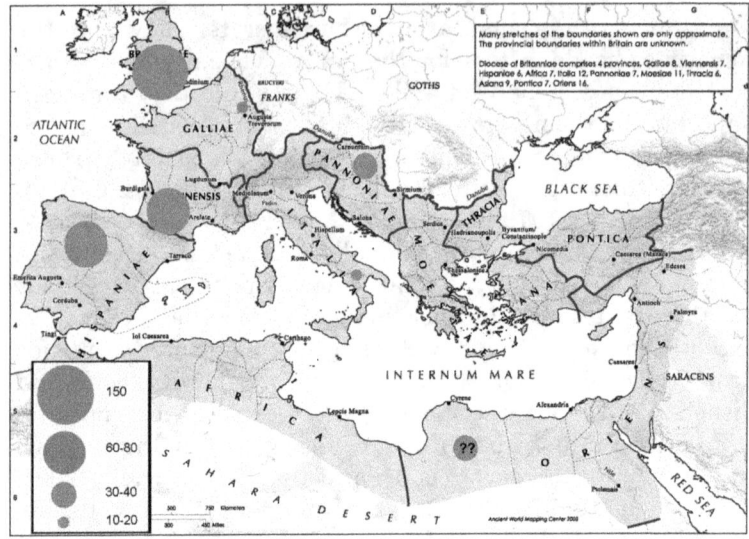

Fig. 21. Map of the Roman empire showing concentrations of monumentalized rural villas.

ever further from cities, clustering along roads. Those roads either led to the Danube frontier with its substantial military apparatus, or served as supply routes behind the frontier. (Mulvin 2002, 11-13, 23, 28-9, 71). The villas themselves often include large granaries, likely intended for military supply.

In Hispania, monumentalized villas are thickest in the underurbanized western and north-central part of the peninsula, clustering in the great river valleys (Chavarría 2007, 40, 93). New research has revealed that the few cities of these regions underwent a spate of new fortification in the late third and early fourth centuries (Fernández Ochoa and Morillo Cerdán 2002; 2005). Aquitaine, thick with villas, similarly saw some of its northern cities fortified in the late third/early fourth century, possibly using military resources and planning (Garmy and Maurin 1996, 18-95). These fortified cities, along with otherwise unexplained legionary presence and the creation of two new, otherwise unexplainable provinces in this area (Gallaecia and Novempopulanie), have been interpreted as evidence for focused

4. New Directions

annona, or military supply collection, destined for the Rhineland frontier. This system, it is argued, was part of a larger Diocletianic reorganization in which the tax-take of the far western provinces was focused ever more tightly on military supply. While it remains unclear if actual goods were being preferentially requisitioned (no Spanish amphora-born products appear in the Rhineland forts in any numbers, for example) or if the collection was largely monetary, the fortified cities, many probably built with military help, were emphatic symbols of imperial/military presence.

In Britain, a similar combination of factors can be identified – a spate of late third-century fortified ports (the so-called Saxon Shore Forts) possibly safeguarding supply routes to the Rhineland estuary, and a heyday of monumental villa-building some decades later. The geography, however, fails to add up – the villas were largely, although not exclusively, focused in the south-west, while the fortified coastal sites and their military/bureaucratic apparatus lay in the south-east (Scott 2000; Fulford 2007). Some resolution may be suggested by a specific late antique ceramic type, the so-called South-Dorset Black Burnished Wares, whose production may have been overseen by provincial or military bureaucracy and whose distribution more or less echoes that of the villas (Allen and Fulford 1996). The functions of this western bureaucratic apparatus are far from clear, but it is possible that its purpose was to organize road-borne cross-island supply chains which connected up with the continental routes departing from the eastern ports (cf. Fulford 2007). As in Hispania, the villas would have been focused at the origins, rather than the termini, of these routes.

Southern Italy, including Sicily, which has thus far produced a thinner corpus of villas, may represent a rather different version of these trends. No evidence of military presence or fortification efforts has been identified. However, after the diversion of Egyptian grain to feed Constantinople and the fifth-century loss of North African territories to the Vandals, the southern Italian provinces had an increasingly important role in the provisioning of Rome. Exciting new work in Puglia is beginning to produce evidence of the administrative apparatus that accompanied that change in status. Epigraphic testimony for imperial estate managers, rural tax collectors, and by the early sixth century, Byzantine armies, now suggest a significant imperial interest in the area (Volpe 2001; Giardina and Grelle 1983; Volpe 2002). Likewise new excavations, field survey and aerial photography are beginning to reveal what may be a major phase of rural building in the same region, including at least some monumentalized villas, like the marble-covered Faragola (Goffredo and Volpe 2005; Romano and Volpe 2007; Volpe 2005).

In sum, we are beginning to see an as-yet vague correlation between hotspots of imperial administration (civilian or military) and concentrations of monumentalized villas. If this were the case, the link between imperial bureaucracy, local elites and villa-construction would be an interesting, albeit complex one. Diocletian's tax reforms tied taxation more firmly to the land itself; the rise of the *iugum*, a land/productivity unit, as preferred measurement of tax liability, and the emphasis on the *origo*, or physical location, of taxpayers, is testament to this (Goffart 1974; Grey 2007). The gaze of not only municipal councillors but now also imperial officials like the *praepositus pagi* or municipal/imperial go-betweens like the *curator rei publicae*, were focused on the site of tax production – the land. In thickly urbanized regions, like west and central North Africa, the bureaucracy of tax would have remained, as it had in centuries past, largely city-bound. In regions without a dense urban network, however, that bureaucracy would have been increasingly felt in the countryside. Rural regions with concentrations of military and imperial bureaucracy, like Pannonia, northern Hispania and southern Britain, thus might have found that same eclectic mixture of elites – local landowners, imperial tax bureaucrats, military men, municipal officials – concentrated in the countryside. The countryside, or at least those regions subject to imperial attention and without cities to focus that attention, might thus have witnessed the same peer-to-peer rivalry that Diocletian and Constantine's reforms unleashed in the

4. New Directions

cities. Villas would thus have served as rurally-based centres of social competition (cf. Scott 2000, 106-7, 112).

Machines for competition

The possible mid-later fourth-century surge in elite house construction, its particular geographies, and the frantic competition among the aristocracy during those years and after – all tentatively suggest an alternative framework for interpreting late antique houses. To rephrase Le Corbusier's dictum, late antique houses may have been machines for competition. Acting as physical sites of *salutatio*, banquets and other moments of social rivalry, or setting off formalistic salvos through the manipulation of a particular architectural language, late antique houses may have performed the social work we regularly attribute to the houses of the late republic and early empire. Such houses may be focused in places where social jostling would have been fiercest, sites where the many different kinds of elites – bureaucrats, *curiales*, military men – converged, and particularly where the lodestone of imperial honours shone the brightest. In these competitive arenas, elites invested their social and economic capital in architecture which could speak for them, could invent them. By employing an iconography of civic architecture and a sophisticated aesthetic language based on curving, apsidal forms, these houses enabled their owners to claw their way up the social ladder.

It was not simply in 'display' – of wealth, of learning – that such houses worked as competitive apparatus. In the suggestive clustering of such houses in a given city or in a particular region lies a conversation, a competitive discourse between neighbouring homeowners. One has only to look at the cluster of villas in the Midi-Pyrénées with their distinctive sigma-shaped courtyards (Fig. 22), or the elaborate water installations of the houses of Djemila, to catch the remnants of these local discourses (Figs 17 and 23). Once the full range of 'elite' houses is folded back into the corpus, this discourse can be traced along a broad socio-economic spectrum. Late Roman houses, in other words, constituted a dialectical architecture, an argument about social belonging, not a mirrored expression of social membership (cf. Woolf 1998. 11).

Neither can these houses be understood as a simple 'reflection' of the Constantinian social reforms. Rather, they are perhaps the most potent evidence for the manipulation of those reforms. The carrot of senatorial status, intended to homogenize aristocratic career paths, produced a stampede for honours that in many ways undermined the emperors' often

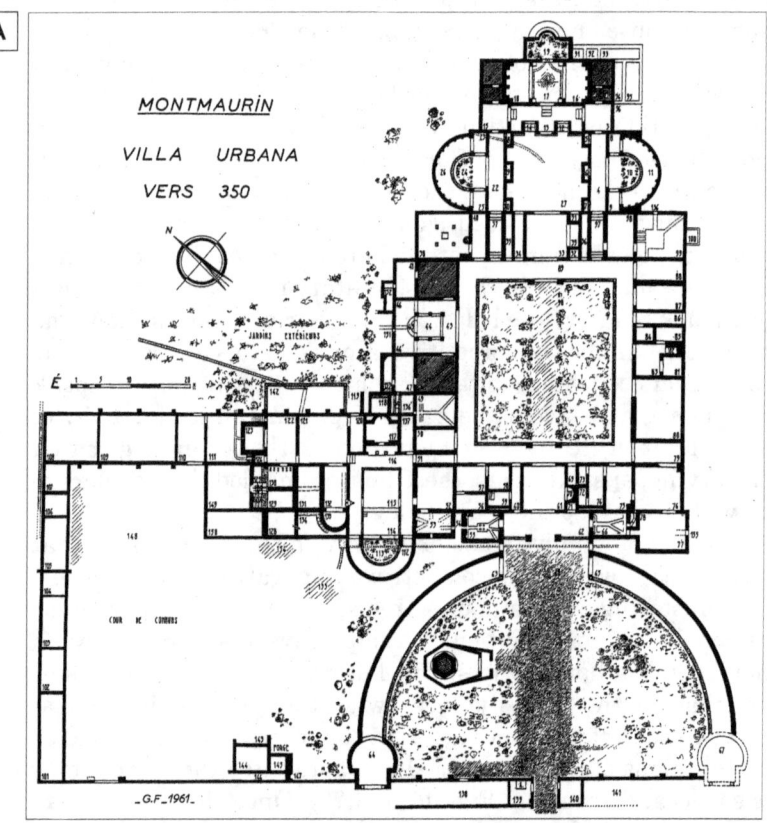

Fig. 22. Some villas of the Midi-Pyrénées/Aquitaine, France. A: Montmaurin; B: Lescar; C: Jurançon.

4. New Directions

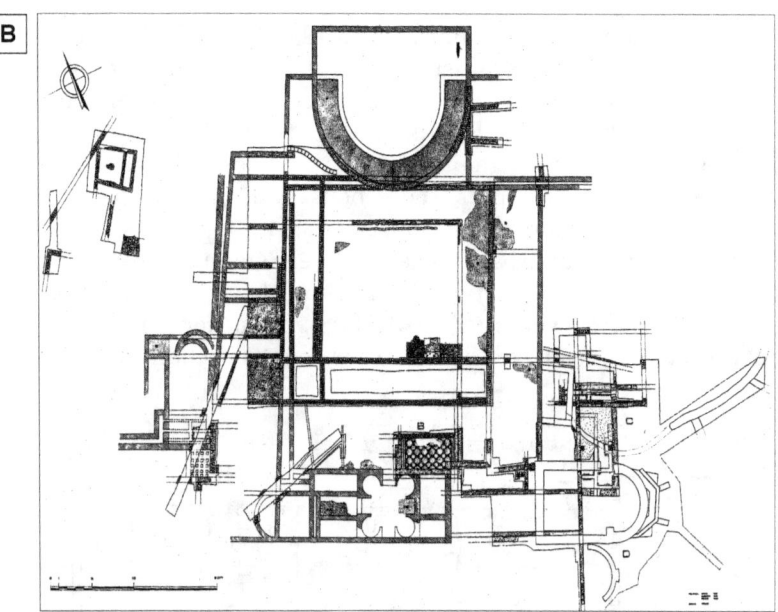

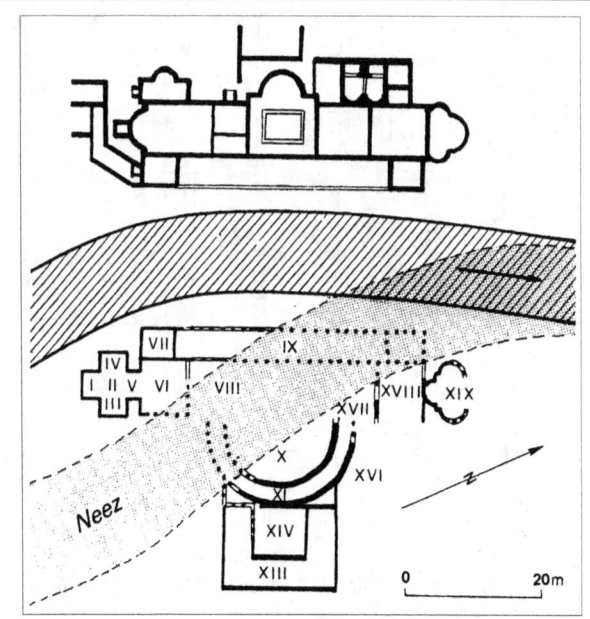

desperate attempts to regularize it (Millar 1983). Houses, like the hundreds of laws against civic-duty-dodging, are the footprints of people in a hurry. Using the age old tactics of personal encounters, shared meals, and the virtuoso deployment of style, their owners sought to grease the wheels of social advancement. In this respect, these houses did not 'reflect' the world of their owners. Like houses from Elvis' Graceland to Tony Soprano's suburban mansion, late Roman houses were tiny pieces of science fiction, calling into being an alternate reality for their owners (cf. Gell 1998). Such houses did not mirror shared social experience – they sought to change it.

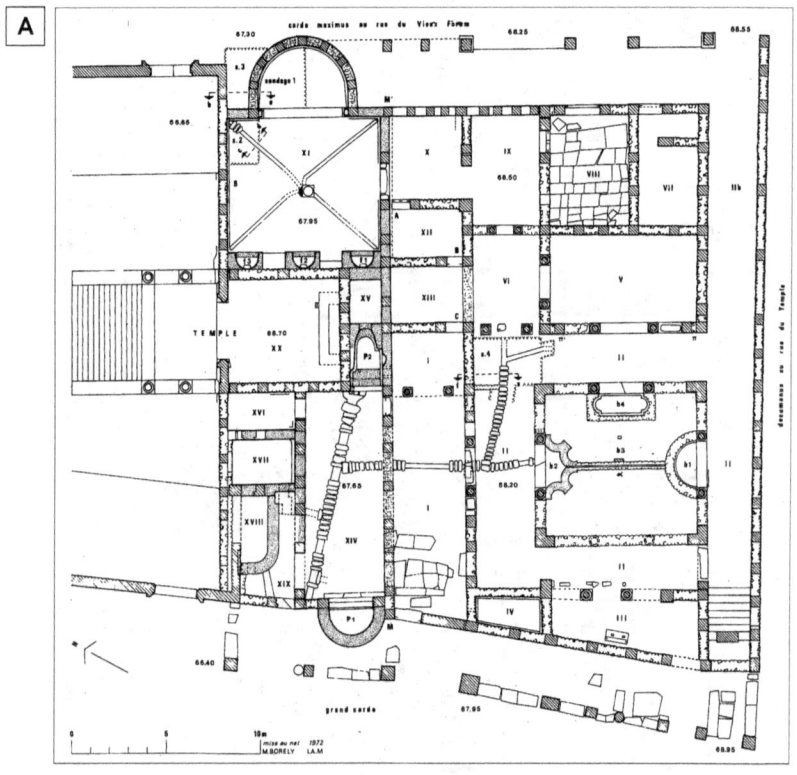

Fig. 23. Houses of Djemila, Tunisia. A: Maison de l'Ane; B: Maison aux Stucs.

4. New Directions

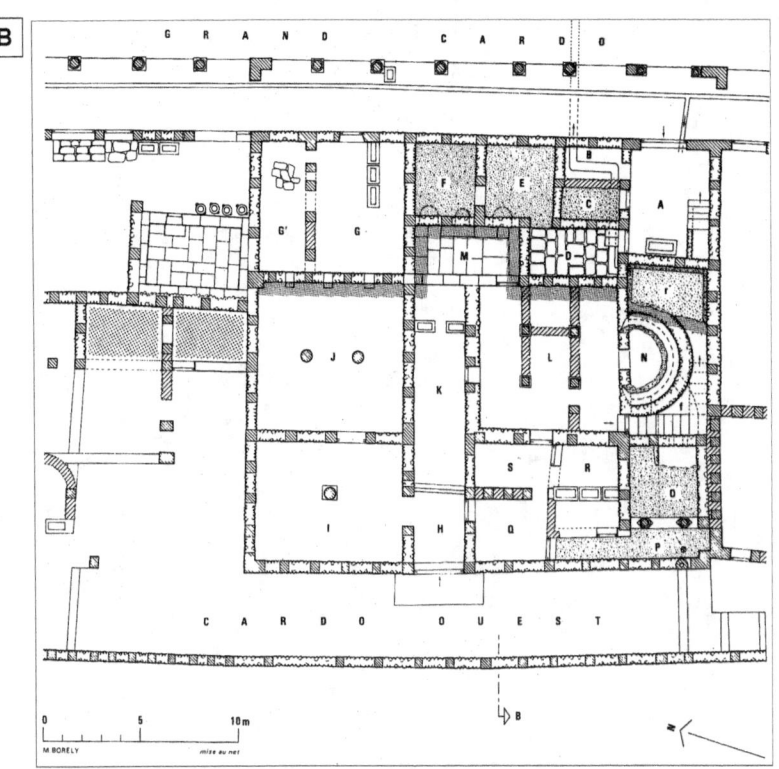

Bibliography

Adam, R., 1764, *Ruins of the Palace of the Emperor Diocletian at Spalato in Dalmatia*, London.
Adamesteanu, D., 1984, 'Sofiana. Scavi 1954 e 1961', in S. Garraffo (ed.) *La villa romana del Casale di Piazza Armerina*, Catania.
Åkerström-Hougen, G., 1974, *The Calendar and Hunting Mosaics of the Villa of the Falconer in Argos*, Stockholm.
Alba Calzado, M., 1997, 'Ocupación diacrónica del área arqueológica de Morería', Merida. *Excavaciones Arqueológicas. Memoria, 1994-5*, 1, 285-301.
Allen, J. and Fulford, M., 1996, 'The distribution of South-East Dorset Black Burnished Category 1 pottery in south-west Britain', *Britannia* 27, 223-81.
Allison, P., 2001, 'Using the material and written sources: turn of the millennium approaches to Roman domestic space', *American Journal of Archaeology* 105, 181-208.
Allison, P., 2004, *Pompeii Households: Analysis of the Material Culture*, Los Angeles.
Allison, P., 2006, 'Engendering Roman spaces', in E. Robertson et al. (eds) *Space and Spatial Analysis in Archaeology*, Calgary, 343-54.
Ault, B. and Nevett, L., 1999, Digging houses: archaeologies of classical and Hellenistic Greek domestic assemblages', in P. Allison (ed.) *The Archaeology of Household Activities*, London, 43-56.
Bagnall, R., 1985, 'Agricultural productivity and taxation in later Roman Egypt', *Transactions of the American Philological Association* 115, 289-308.
Baldini Lippolis, I., 2002, *La domus tardoantica: forme e rappresentazioni dello spazio domestico nelle citta del Mediterraneo*, Bologna.
Balmelle, C., 2001, *Les demeures aristocratiques d'Aquitaine: société et culture de l'antiquité tardive dans le Sud-Ouest de la Gaule*, Bordeaux.
Balty, J., 1997, Mosaïque et architecture domestique dans l'Apamée

Bibliography

des Ve et VIe s', in S. Isager and B. Poulson (eds) *Patrons and Pavements in Late Antiquity*, Odense, 84-110.

Banaji, J., 1997, 'Lavoratori liberi e residenza coatta: il colonato romano in prospectiva storica', in E. Lo Cascio (ed.) *Terre, proprietari e contadini dell'impero romano*, Rome, 253-80.

Banaji, J., 2001, *Agrarian Change in Late Antiquity: Gold, Labour and Aristocratic Dominance*, Oxford.

Barker, G. (ed.), 1996, *Farming the Desert: The UNESCO Libyan Valley Archaeological Survey*, Paris/Tripoli/London.

Becatti, G., 1948, 'Case ostiensi del tardo impero', *Bollettino d'Arte* 33, 102-22.

Bek, L., 1983, '*Questiones Convivales*: the idea of the triclinium and the staging of convivial ceremony from Rome to Byzantium', *Analecta Romana Instituti Danici* 12, 81-107.

Berenfeld, M., 2002, 'The Bishop's Palace at Aphrodisias: a late antique townhouse transformed, AD 400-1200', PhD Thesis, Institute of Fine Arts, New York University.

Berry, J., 1997, 'Household artifacts: towards a re-interpretation of Roman domestic space', in R. Laurence and A. Wallace-Hadrill (eds) *Domestic Space in the Roman World, Pompeii and Beyond*, Portsmouth, RI, 183-96.

Beschaouch, A., Hanoune, R. and Thébert, Y., 1977, *Les ruines de Bulla Regia*, Rome.

Beylié, L.D., 1902, *L'habitation byzantine*, Grenoble/Paris.

Bianchi Bandinelli, R., 1971, *Rome. The Late Empire. Roman Art AD 200-400*, London.

Black, E.W., 1987, *The Roman Villas of South-East England*, Oxford.

Blanchard-Lemée, H., 1975, *Maisons à mosaïques du quartier central de Djemila Cuicul*, Paris.

Blanchard-Lemée, H., 1981, 'La maison de Bacchus à Djemila', *Bulletin d'archéologie algérienne* 17, 131-41.

Blanton, R., 1994, *Houses and Households: A Comparative Study*, New York/London.

Bourdieu, P., 1977, *Outline of a Theory of Practice*, Cambridge.

Bowden, W. forthcoming, 'Elite architecture and space in late antique Butrint', in W. Bowden and R. Hodges, *The Triconch Palace in Butrint*, Oxford.

Bowden, W. and Mitchell, J., 2007, 'The Triconch Palace at Butrint: life and death of a late Roman *domus*', in L. Lavan, L. Özgenel and A. Sarantis (eds) *Housing in Late Antiquity: From Palaces to Shops*, Leiden, 455-74.

Bibliography

Bowman, A.K., 1980, 'The economy of Egypt in the earlier fourth century AD', in C. King (ed.) *Imperial Revenue, Expenditure and Monetary Policy in the Fourth Century AD*, Oxford, 23-40.

Brenk, B., 1999, 'La cristianizzazione della Domus dei Valerii sul Celio', in W.V. Harris (ed.) *The Transformations of URBS ROMA in Late Antiquity*, Portsmouth, RI, 69-84.

Brogiolo, G. and Gelichi, S.,1998, *La cittá nell'alto medioevo italiano*, Rome/Bari.

Brown, P., 1971, 'The rise and function of the holy man in late antiquity', *Journal of Roman Studies* 61, 80-101.

Bullo, S. and Ghedini, F., 2003, *Amplissimae atque ornatissimae domus. L'edilizia residenziale nelle città della Tunisia romana*, Rome.

Burton, G.P., 1979, 'The curator rei publicae: towards a reappraisal', *Chiron* 9, 465-87.

Cahill, N., 2002, *Household and City Organization at Olynthus*, New Haven.

Cambi, F. et al., 1994, 'Etruria, Tuscia, Toscana: la formazione di paesaggi altomedievali', in R. Francovich and G. Noyé (eds) *La Storia dell'Alto Medioevo italiano (VI-X secolo) alla luce dell'archeologia*, Florence, 183-215.

Capogrossi Colognesi, L., 1986, 'Grandi proprietari, contadini e coloni nell'Italia romana (I-III d.c.)', in A. Giardina (ed.) *Società romana e impero tardoantico*, Rome/Bari, 325-65.

Carandini, A., 1985, 'Da villa perfecta', in A. Carandini (ed.) *Settefinestre, una villa schiavistica nell'Etruria Romana*, Modena, 107-37.

Carandini, A., 1989, 'La villa romana e la piantagione schiavistica', in A. Momigliano and A. Schiavone, *Storia di Roma*, vol. 4: *Caratteri e morofologie*, Turin, 101-30.

Carandini, A., Ricci, A. and De Vos, M., 1982, *Filosofiana, la villa di Piazza Armerina: immagine di un aristocratico romano al tempo di Costantino*, Palermo.

Carrié, J.-M., 1976, 'Patronage et propriété militaires au IVe siècle: objet rhétorique et objet réel du discours, Sur les patronages de Libanius', *Bulletin de correspondence hellénique* 100, 159-79.

Carrié, J.-M., 1982, 'Le "colonat du Bas-Empire": un mythe historiographique?', *Opus* 1, 351-70.

Carrié, J.-M., 1983, 'Un roman des origines', *Opus* 2, 205-51.

Carrié, J.-M., 1997, ' "Colonato basso imperio": la resistenza del mito', in E. Lo Cascio (ed.) *Terre, propietari e contadini dell'impero romano*, Bari, 75-150.

Bibliography

Carrié, J.-M., 2005, 'Developments in provincial and local administration', in A. Bowman, P. Garnsey and A. Cameron (eds) *Cambridge Ancient History*, vol. 12: *The Crisis of Empire*, 2nd edn, Cambridge, 269-312.

Castrén, P., 1994, 'General aspects of life in post-Herulian Athens', in P. Castrén (ed.) *Post-Herulian Athens: Aspects of Life and Culture in Athens, AD 267-529*, Helsinki, 1-14.

Ceylan, B., 2007, 'Episkopeia in Asia Minor', in L. Lavan, L. Özgenel and A. Sarantis (eds) *Housing in Late Antiquity: From Palaces to Shops*, Leiden, 169-94.

Chavarría, A., 2005, 'Villas in Hispania during the fourth and fifth centuries', in K. Bowes and M. Kulikowski (eds) *Hispania in Late Antiquity: Current Perspectives* Leiden, 519-52.

Chavarría, A., 2007, *El final de las villae en Hispania (siglos IV-VII D.C.)*, Turnhout.

Conybeare, C., 2000, Paulinus Noster: *Self and Symbols in the Letters of Paulinus of Nola*, Oxford.

Cromley, E., 2003, 'Domestic space transformed, 1850-2000', in A. Ballantyne (ed.) *Architectures: Modernism and After*, London, 163-201.

Ćurčić, S., 1993, 'Late antique palaces: the meaning of urban context', *Ars Orientalis*, 23, 67-90.

DiSegni, L., 1995, 'The involvement of local, municipal and provincial authorities in urban building in late antique Palestine', in J. Humphrey (ed.) *The Roman and Byzantine Near East: Some Recent Archaeological Research*, Ann Arbor, MI, 312-32.

Duby, G., Barthélemy, D. and Roncière, C.D.L., 1988, 'The aristocratic households of feudal France', in G. Duby (ed.) *A History of Private Life: Revelations of the Medieval World*, Cambridge, MA, 35-155.

Dunbabin, K., 1991, 'Triclinium and stibadium', in W. Slater (ed.) *Dining in a Classical Context*, Ann Arbor, 121-48.

Duncan-Jones, R., 1990. *Structure and Scale in the Roman Economy*, Cambridge.

Duval, N., 1961, 'Le probleme de l'architecture aulique au bas-empire', *Atti del settimo congresso internazionale di archeologia classica*, Rome, 2, 407-10.

Duval, N., 1978, 'Comment reconnaitre un palais imperial ou royal? Ravenne et Piazza Armerina', *Felix Ravenna* 115, 29-62.

Duval, N., 1984, 'Les maisons d'Apamée et l'architecture "palatiale" de l'antiquité tardive', in J. Balty (ed.) *Apamée de Syrie. Bilan des recherches archéologiques 1973-1979*, Brussels, 447-70.

Bibliography

Duval, N., 1997, 'Les résidences impériales: leur rapport avec les problèmes de légitimité, les partages de l'Empire et la chronologie des combinaisons dynastiques', in F. Paschoud and J. Szidat (eds) *Usurpationen in der Spätantike*, Stuttgart, 127-53.

Dyggve, E., 1941, *Ravennatum Palatium Sacrum*, Copenhagen.

Dyggve, E., 1956, 'Basilica Herculis', *Festschrift W. Sas-Zaloziecky zum 60. Geburtstag*, Graz, 34-9.

Dyggve, E., 1961, 'Contributo alla discussione sul "Palatium-Ecclesia"', *Atti del settimo congresso internazionale di archeologia classica*. Rome, 401-6.

Ellis, S., 1985. 'The "Palace of the Dux" at Apollonia and related houses', in G. Barker, J. Lloyd and J. Reynolds (eds) *Cyrenaica in Antiquity*, London, 15-25.

Ellis, S., 1988, 'The end of the Roman house', *American Journal of Archaeology* 92, 565-76.

Ellis, S., 1991, 'Power, architecture and decor: how the late Roman aristocrat appeared to his guests', in E. Gazda (ed.) *Roman Art in the Private Sphere*, Ann Arbor, 117-34.

Ellis, S., 1997a, 'Late-antique dining: architecture, furnishings and behaviour', in R. Laurence and A. Wallace-Hadrill (eds) *Domestic Space in the Roman World: Pompeii and Beyond*, Portsmouth, RI, 41-51.

Ellis, S., 1997b, 'Late antique houses in Asia Minor', in S. Isager and B. Poulsen (eds) *Patron and Pavements in Late Antiquity*, Odense, 38-50.

Ellis, S., 2007, 'Late antique housing and the uses of residential buildings: an overview', in L. Lavan, L. Özgenel and A. Sarantis (eds) *Housing in Late Antiquity: From Palaces to Shops*, Leiden, 1-22.

Elsner, J., 1995, *Art and the Roman Viewer*, Cambridge.

Engemann, J., 1982, 'Der Ehrenplatz beim antiken Sigmamahl', *Jenseitsvorstellungen in Antike und Christentum. Gedenkschrift fur Alfred Stuiber*, Münster, 239-50.

Etienne, R., 1960, *Le quartier nord-est de Volubilis*, Paris.

Fabbricotti, E., 1976, 'I bagni nella prime ville romane', *Cronache Pompeiane* 2, 29-111.

Fagan, G., 1999, *Bathing in Public in the Roman World*, Ann Arbor.

Fernández-Galiano, D. (ed.), 2001, *Carranque. Centro de Hispania romana*, Alcalá de Henares.

Fernández Ochoa, C. and Morillo Cerdán, Á., 2002, 'Entre el prestigio y la defensa: la problematica estratègico-defensiva de las murallas tardorromanas en Hispania', in Á. Morillo Cerdán (ed.) *Arqueología militar romana en Hispania*, Madrid, 577-89.

Fernández Ochoa, C. and Morillo Cerdán, Á., 2005, 'Walls in the urban landscape of late Roman Spain: defense and imperial strategy', in K. Bowes and M. Kulikowski (eds) *Hispania in Late Antiquity: Current Approaches*, Leiden, 299-340.

Fernoux, H.-L., 2004, *Notables et élites des cités de Bithynie aux époques hellénistique et romaine*, Lyon.

Foss, C., 1979, *Ephesus after Antiquity: A Late Antique, Byzantine and Turkish City*, Cambridge.

Frantz, A., 1988, *The Athenian Agora, XXIV. Late Antiquity, AD 267-700*, Princeton.

Fulford, M., 2007, 'Coasting Britannia: Roman trade and traffic around the shores of Britain', in C. Gosden et al. (eds) *Communities and Connections: Essays in Honour of Barry Cunliffe*, Oxford, 54-74.

Garmy, P. and Maurin, L., 1996, *Enceintes romaines d'Aquitaine*, Documents d'archéologie française 53, Paris.

Garnsey, P. and Whittaker, C., 1998, 'Trade, industry and the urban economy', in A. Cameron and P. Garnsey (eds) *Cambridge Ancient History*, vol. XIII: *The Late Empire 337-345*, Cambridge, 312-37.

Garnsey, P. and Woolf, G., 1989, 'Patronage of the rural poor', in A. Wallace-Hadrill (ed.) *Patronage in Ancient Society*, London/New York, 153-70.

Gascou, J., 1976, 'Les institutions de l'hippodrome en Égypte byzantine', *Bulletin de l'Institute français d'archéólogie orientale* 76, 185-212.

Geertz, C., 1983, 'Art as a cultural system', *Local Knowledge: Further Essays in Interpretive Anthropology*, New York, 94-120.

Gell, A., 1998, *Art and Agency*, Oxford.

Gentili, G.V., 1951, *La villa imperiale di Piazza Armerina*, Rome.

Gentili, G.V., 1999, *La villa romana di Piazza Armerina. Palazzo Erculio*, Osimo.

Gering, A., 2004, 'Plätze und Straßensperren an Promenaden. Zum Funktionswandel Ostias in der Spätantike', *Mitteilungen des Deutschen Archäologischen Instituts, Römische Abteilung* 111, 299-381.

Ghedini, F., 2003, 'La casa romana in Tunisia tra tradizione e innovazione', in S. Bullo and F. Ghedini (eds) *Amplissimae atque ornatissimae domus: l'edilizia residenziale nelle città della Tunisia romana*, Rome, 315-56.

Ghiotto, A., 2003. 'Gli impianti termali', in S. Bullo and F. Ghedini

Bibliography

(eds) *Amplissimae atque ornatissimae domus: l'edilizia residenziale nelle città della Tunisia romana*, Rome, 221-32.

Giardina, A. and Grelle, F., 1983, 'La tavola di Trinitapoli: una nuova costituzione di Valentiniano I', *Mélanges de l'École Française de Rome: Antiquité* 95, 249-303.

Giardina, A. and Schiavone, A. (eds), 1981, *Societa' romana e produzione schiavistica*, Bari.

Gieryn, T., 2002, 'What buildings do', *Theory and Society* 31, 35-74.

Gilkes, O.J. and Lako, K., 2004, 'Excavations at the Triconch Palace', in R. Hodges, W. Bowden and K. Lako (eds) *Byzantine Butrint: Excavations and Survey 1994-1999*, Oxford, 151-75.

Goffart, W., 1974, *Caput and Colonate: Towards a History of Late Roman Taxation*, Toronto.

Goffredo, R. and Volpe, G., 2005, 'Il "Progetto Valle dell'Ofanto": primi dati sulla tarda antichità e l'altomedioevo', in G. Volpe and M. Turchiano (eds) *Paesaggi e insediamenti rurali in Italia meridionale fra Tardoantico e Altomedioevo*, Bari, 223-40.

Goodchild, R., 1976, 'The "Palace of the Dux" ', in J. Humphrey (ed.) *Apollonia, the Port of Cyrene: Excavations Conducted by the University of Michigan 1965-1967*, Tripoli, 245-65.

Gorges, J.-G., 1979, *Les villas hispano-romaines*, Paris.

Graham, J.W., 1966, 'Origins and interrelations of the Greek house and the Roman house', *Phoenix* 20, 3-31.

Grahame, M., 2000, *Reading Space: Social Interaction and Identity in the Houses of Roman Pompeii. A Syntactical Approach to the Analysis and Interpretation of Built Space*, Oxford.

Grey, C., 2007, 'Contextualizing *colonatus*: the *origo* of the late Roman empire', *Journal of Roman Studies* 97, 155-75.

Gros, P., 2004, 'La basilique dans la maison des notables', in M. CeBeillac-Gervasoni, L. Lamoine and F.D.R. TreMent (eds) *Autocelebration des elites locales dans le monde romain: contextes, images, textes, IIe s. av. J.-C.-IIIe s. ap. J.-C*, Clermont-Ferrand, 311-39.

Guidobaldi, F., 1986, 'L'edilizia abitativa unifamiliare nella Roma tardoantica', in A. Giardina (ed.) *Società romana e impero tardoantico II: Roma. Politica, economia, paesaggio urbano*, Rome/Bari, 165-237.

Guidobaldi, F., 1993, 'Roma. Il tessuto abitativo, le "domus" e i "tituli" ', in A. Carandini, L. Cracco Ruggini and A. Giardina (eds) *Storia di Roma. III: L'età tardoantica. 2: I luoghi e le culture*, Turin, 69-83.

Guidobaldi, F., 1999, 'Le domus tardo antiche di Roma come "sensori" delle trasformazioni culturali e sociali', in W.V. Harris (ed.) *The Transformations of the URBS ROMA in Late Antiquity*, Portsmouth, RI, 53-68.

Hales, S., 2003, *The Roman House and Social Identity*, Cambridge.

Harmand, L., 1955, *Discours sur les patronages*, Paris.

Heather, P., 1998, 'Senators and senates', in A. Cameron and P. Garnsey (eds) *Cambridge Ancient History*, vol. 13: *The Late Empire AD 337-425*, Cambridge, 184-210.

Hellman, C., 2004, 'The other American kitchen: alternative domesticity in 1950s design, politics, and fiction', *Americana* 3, http://www.americanpopularculture.com/journal/articles/fall_2004/hellman.htm.

Henderson, J., 2004, *Morals and Villas in Seneca's Letters*, Oxford.

Hoepfner, W. and Schwandner, E.-L., 1986, *Haus und Stadt im klassischen Griechenland*, Munich.

Hölscher, T., 2004, *The Language of Images in Roman Art*, Cambridge.

Hopkins, K., 1965, 'Social mobility in the Roman empire', *Past and Present* 32, 12-26.

Jacques, F., 1986, 'L'ordine senatorio attraverso la crisi del III secolo', *Societá romana e impero tardoantico I: Istituzioni, ceti, economie*, Rome/Bari, 81-225.

Jilek, S., 2005, 'Kleinfunde aus Metal und Bein', in H. Thür (ed.) *Hanghaus 2 in Ephesos. Die Wohneinheit 4*, Vienna, 389-413.

Jones, A.H.M., 1959, 'Over-taxation and the decline of the Roman empire', *Antiquity* 33, 39-43.

Jones, A.H.M., 1964, *The Later Roman Empire*, Baltimore.

Kaster, R., 1988, *Guardians of Language: The Grammarian and Society in Late Antiquity*, Berkeley.

Kehoe, D., 2007, 'The early Roman empire: production', in W. Scheidel, I. Morris and R. Saller (eds) *Cambridge Economic History of the Greco-Roman World*, Cambridge, 543-69.

Keil, J., 1932, 'XVI. Vorläufiger Bericht über der Ausgrabungen in Ephesos', *Jahreshefte des Österreichischen Archäologischen Instituts* 27, Beiblatt (2), 5-72.

Kelly, C., 2004, *Ruling the Late Roman Empire*, Berkeley.

Keuls, E., 1985, *The Reign of the Phallus*, New York.

King, A., 2000, 'Thinking with Bourdieu against Bourdieu: a "practical" critique of the habitus', *Sociological Theory* 18, 417-33.

Kotula, T., 1982, *Les principales d'Afrique: étude sur l'élite municipale nord-africaine au bas-empire romain*, Warsaw.

Bibliography

Krause, J.-U., 1987, *Spätantike Patronatsformen im Westen des römischen Reiches*, Munich.
Krautheimer, R., 1969, 'The beginning of early Christian architecture', *Studies in Early Christian, Medieval and Renaissance Art*, New York, 1-20.
Kulikowski, M., 2004, *Late Roman Spain and its Cities*, Baltimore/London.
L'Orange, H.P., 1965, *Art Forms and Civic Life in the Later Roman Empire*, Princeton.
Ladstätter, S., 2005, 'Keramik', in H. Thür (ed.) *Hanghaus 2 in Ephesos. Die Wohneinheit 4*, Vienna, 230-62.
Lang-Auinger, C., 1996, *Hanghaus 1 in Ephesos: Der Baubefund*, Vienna.
Laniado, A., 2002, *Recherches sur les notables municipaux dans l'Empire protobyzantin*, Paris.
Lavan, L., 2001a, 'Provincial capitals of late antiquity', PhD, University of Nottingham.
Lavan, L. (ed.), 2001b, *Recent Research in Late-Antique Urbanism*, Portsmouth.
Lavan, L., 2003, 'Christianity, the city and the end of antiquity', *Journal of Roman Archaeology* 16, 705-10.
Lavan, L., Özgenel, L. and Sarantis, A. (eds) (2007) *Housing in Late Antiquity: From Palaces to Shops*, Leiden.
Lavin, I., 1962, 'The house of the lord: aspects of the role of palace triclinia in the architecture of late antiquity and the early Middle Ages', *Art Bulletin* 44, 1-27.
LeBohec, Y., 2005, *Histoire de l'Afrique romaine, 146 avant J.-C.- 439 après J.-C.*, Paris.
LeBohec, Y., 2007, 'L'armée romaine d'Afrique de 375 à 439', in A. Lewin and P. Pellegrini (eds) *The Late Roman Army in the Near East from Diocletian to the Arab Conquest*, Oxford, 431-41.
Lehmann, C.M. and Holum, K., 2000, *The Greek and Latin Inscriptions of Caesarea Maritima*, Boston.
Lepelley, C., 1979-81, *Les cités de l'Afrique romaine au Bas-Empire. I. La permanence d'une civilization municipal*, Paris.
Lepelley, C., 1986, 'Fine dell'ordine equestre: le tappe dell'unificazione della classe dirigente romana nel IV secolo', in A. Giardina (ed.) *Società romana e imperio tardoantico*, vol. 1: *Istituzioni, ceti, economie*, Rome/Bari, 227-44.
Lewin, A. and Pellegrini, P. (eds) (2006) *Settlements and Demography in the Near East in Late Antiquity*, Pisa.

Bibliography

Lewit, T., 1991, *Agricultural Production in the Roman Economy AD 200-400*, Oxford.

Liebenam, W., 1897, 'Curator rei publicae', *Philologus* 56, 290-335.

Liebeschuetz, J.H.W.G., 1972, *Antioch: City and Imperial Administration in the Later Roman Empire*, Oxford.

Liebeschuetz, J.H.W.G., 2001, *The Decline and Fall of the Roman City*, Oxford.

Liebeschuetz, J.H.W.G., 2006, 'Transformation and decline: are the two really incompatible?', in J.-U. Krause and C. Witschel (eds) *Die Stadt in der Spätantike – Niedergang oder Wandel?*, Stuttgart, 463-83.

MacMullen, R., 1964, 'Social mobility and the Theodosian Code', *Journal of Roman Studies* 54, 49-53.

MacMullen, R., 1988, *Corruption and the Decline of Rome*, New Haven.

Manière-Lévêque, A.-M., 2007, 'The House of the Lycian Acropolis at Xanthos', in L. Lavan, L. Özgenel and A. Sarantis (eds) *Housing in Late Antiquity: From Palaces to Shops*, Leiden, 473-94.

Marcone, A., 1998, 'Late Roman social relations', in A. Cameron and P. Garnsey (eds) *Cambridge Ancient History*, vol. XIII: *The Late Empire 337-345*, Cambridge, 338-70.

Marquardt, J. and Mau, A., 1886, *Das Privatleben der Römer*, Rome.

Martin, R., 1995, 'Les sources littéraires de la notion de *latifundium*', in *De latifundium au latifondo*, Paris, 97-106.

Marzano, A., 2007, *Roman Villas in Central Italy: A Social and Economic History* Leiden.

Mau A., 1894-, 'Convivium', in Pauly-Wissowa, *Real-Encyclopädie der klassischen Altertumswissenschaft* 7, 1201-8.

Mau, A., 1899, *Pompeii: Its Life and Art*, New York.

Meiggs, R., 1960, *Roman Ostia*, Oxford.

Millar, F., 1983, 'Empire and city, Augustus to Julian: obligations, excuses and status', *Journal of Roman Studies* 73, 76-96.

Miltner, F., 1956, 'XXI Vorläufiger Bericht über die Ausgrabungen in Ephesos', *Jahreshefte des Österreichischen Archäologischen Instituts in Wein* 43, Beiblatt, 2-63.

Miltner, F., 1959, 'XXII Vorläufiger Bericht über die Ausgrabungen in Ephesos', *Jahreshefte des Österreichischen Archäologischen Instituts* 44, Beiblatt, 243-314.

Mirkovic, M., 1997, *The Later Roman Colonate and Freedom*, Philadelphia.

Morand, I., 1994, *Idéologie, culture et spiritualité chez les propriétaires ruraux de l'Hispanie romaine*, Paris.

Bibliography

Mouritsen, H., 1988, *Elections, Magistrates and Municipal Élite: Studies in Pompeiian Epigraphy*, Rome.

Mulvin, L., 2002, *Late Roman Villas in the Danube-Balkan Region*, Oxford.

Navarro Sáez, R., 1999, 'Vil.la Fortunatus', in *Del Romà al Romànic*, Barcelona, 146-50.

Neeve, P.W.D., 1984, *Colonus: Private Farm-Tenancy in Roman Italy during the Republic and the Early Principate*, Amsterdam.

Nevett, L., 1999, *House and Society in the Ancient Greek World*, Cambridge.

Özgenel, L., 2007, 'The architecture of spatial control', in L. Lavan, L. Özgenel and A. Sarantis (eds) *Housing in Late Antiquity: From Palaces to Shops*, Leiden, 239-81.

Pace, B., 1955, *Mosaici di Piazza Armerina*, Rome.

Palme, B., 1999, 'Die *officia* der Statthalter in der Spätantike. Forschungsstand und Perspektiven', *Antiquité tardive* 7, 85-133.

Patterson, J., 2006, *Landscapes and Cities: Rural Settlement and Civic Transformation in Early Imperial Italy*, Oxford.

Pavolini, C., 1986, 'L'edilizia commerciale e l'edilizia abitativa nel contesto di Ostia tardoanica', in A. Giardina (ed.) *Società romana e impero tardoantico II: Roma. Politica, economia, paesaggio urbano*, Rome/Bari, 239-97.

Perring, D., 2003, 'Aristocratic houses of Aquitaine in late antiquity', *Journal of Roman Archaeology* 16, 701-4.

Petit, P., 1955, *Libanius et la vie municale à Antioche au IVe siècle aprés J.-C.*, Paris.

Polci, B., 2003, 'Some aspects of the transformation of the Roman domus between late antiquity and the early Middle Ages', in L. Lavan and W. Bowden (eds) *Theory and Practice in Late Antique Archaeology*, Leiden, 79-109.

Putzeys, T. et al., 2004, 'Analyzing domestic contexts at Sagalassos: developing a methodology using ceramics and macro-botanical remains', *Journal of Mediterranean Archaeology* 17, 31-57.

Rapoport, A., 1969, *House Form and Culture*, Englewood Cliffs, NJ.

Ratté, C., 2001, 'The urban development of Aphrodisias in late antiquity', in D. Parrish (ed.) *Urbanism in Western Asia Minor*, Portsmouth, RI, 117-47.

Riggsby, A., 1997, ' "Public" and "private" in Roman culture: the case of the *cubiculum*', *Journal of Roman Archaeology* 10, 36-56.

Roberts, M., 1989, *The Jeweled Style: Poetry and Poetics in Late Antiquity*, Ithaca.

Bibliography

Romano, A.V. and Volpe, G., 2007, 'Paesaggi e insediamenti rurali nel comprensorio del Celone fra Tardoantico e Altomedioevo', in G. Volpe and M. Turchiano (eds) *Paesaggi e insediamenti rurali in Italia meridionale fra Tardoantico e Altomedioevo*, Bari, 241-59.

Romizzi, L., 2006, 'Le ville tardo-antiche in Italia', in A. Chavarría, G.P. Brogiolo and J. Arce (eds) *Villas tardoantiguas en el mediterráneo occidental*, Madrid, 37-59.

Rostovtzeff, M.,1910, *Studien zur Geschichte des romischen Kolonates*, Leipzig/Berlin.

Rostovtzeff, M., 1926, *The Social and Economic History of the Roman Empire*, Oxford.

Roueché, C., 1979. A new inscription from Aphrodisias and the title patêr tês poleôs', *Greek, Roman and Byzantine Studies* 20, 173-85.

Roueché, C., 1989a, *Aphrodisias in Late Antiquity*, London.

Roueché, C., 1989b, 'Floreat Perge', in M. Mackenzie and C. Roueché (eds) *Images of Authority: Papers Presented to Joyce Reynolds on the Occasion of her 70th Birthday*, Cambridge, 215-21.

Roueché, C., 1998, 'The functions of the governor in late antiquity: some observations', *Antiquité Tardive* 6, 31-6.

Saller, R., 1982, *Personal Patronage under the Early Empire*, Cambridge.

Salzman, M., 2002, *The Making of a Christian Aristocracy: Social and Religious Change in the Western Roman Empire*, Cambridge, MA.

Sarris, P., 2004, 'Rehabilitating the great estate: aristocratic property and economic growth in the late antique East', in W. Bowden, L. Lavan and C. Machado (eds) *Recent Research on the Late Antique Countryside*, Leiden, 55-71.

Sartre-Fauriat, A., 2003, 'Les élites de la Syrie intérieure et leur image à l'époque romaine', in M. CeBeillac-Gervasoni and L. Lamoine (eds) *Les élites et leurs facettes: les élites locales dans le monde hellenistique et romain*, Rome, 517-38.

Scheidel, W., 2000, 'Slaves of the soil', *Journal of Roman Archaeology* 13, 727-32.

Scherrer, P., 1995, 'The city of Ephesos from the Roman period to late antiquity', in H. Koester (ed.) *Ephesos, Metropolis of Asia*, Valley Forge, PA, 1-25.

Schneider, L., 1983, *Die Domäne als Weltbild: Wirkungsstrukturen der spätantiken Bildersprache*, Weisbaden.

Schweizer, J., 2005, *Baukörper und Raum in tetrarchischer und konstantinischer Zeit*, Bern.

Bibliography

Scott, S., 2000, *Art and Society in Fourth-Century Britain: Villa Mosaics in Context*, Oxford.

Scott, S., 2004, 'Elites, exhibitionism and the society of the late Roman villa', in N. Christie (ed.) *Landscapes of Change: Rural Evolutions in Late Antiquity and the Early Middle Ages*, Aldershot, 39-65.

Seek, O., 1901, *Geschichte des Untergangs der antiken Welt*, Berlin.

Seek, O., 1910, 'Decemprimat und Dekaprotie', *Klio*, 147-87.

Sessa, K., 2007, 'Christianity and the *cubiculum*: spiritual politics and domestic space in late antique Rome', *Journal of Early Christian Studies* 15, 171-204.

Settis, S., 1975, 'Per l'interpretazione di Piazza Amerina', *Mélanges de l'École Française de Rome: Antiquité* 87, 873-994.

Sfameni, C., 2006a, 'Committenza e funzioni delle ville "residenziali" tardoantiche tra fonti archeologiche e fonti letterarie', in A. Chavarría, G.P. Brogiolo and J. Arce (eds) *Villas tardoantiguas en el mediterráneo occidental*, Madrid, 61-72.

Sfameni, C., 2006b, *Ville residenziali nell'Italia tardoantica*, Bari.

Sironen, E., 1994, 'Life and administration of late Roman Attica', in P. Castrén (ed.) *Post-Herulian Athens: Aspects of Life and Culture in Athens AD 267-529*, Helsinki, 15-62.

Smith, R. and Bugni, V., 2006, 'Symbolic interaction theory and architecture', *Symbolic Interaction* 29, 123-55.

Sodini, J.-P., 1995, 'Habitat de l'antiquité tardive', *Topoi. Orient-Occident* 5, 151-218.

Sodini, J.-P., 1997, 'Habitat de l'antiquité tardive (2)', *Topoi. Orient-Occident* 7, 435-575.

Stevens, C.E., 1966, 'The social and economic apsects of rural settlement', in C. Thomas (ed.) *Rural Settlement in Roman Britain*, London, 108-30.

Strube, C., 1973, 'Der begriff *domus* in der Notitia Urbis Constantinopolitanae', in H. Beck (ed.) *Studien zur Frühgeschichte Konstantinopels*, Munich, 121-34.

Swoboda, K., 1919, *Römische und romanische Paläste*, Vienna.

Tamm, B., 1963, *Auditorium and Palatium: A Study on Assembly-rooms in Roman Palaces during the 1st Century BC and the 1st Century AD*, Stockholm.

Tchalenko, G., 1953-59, *Villages antiques de la Syrie du Nord*, Paris.

Thébert, Y., 1987, 'Private life and domestic architecture in Roman Africa', in P. Veyne (ed.) *A History of Private Life: From Pagan Rome to Byzantium*, Cambridge, MA, 313-410.

Bibliography

Thébert, Y., 1988. 'À propos du "triomphe du christianisme" ', *Dialogues d'Histoire Ancienne* 15, 277-345.

Thébert, Y., 2003, *Thermes romains d'afrique du nord et leur context méditerranéen*, Rome.

Thür, H., 1996, 'Die spätantike Bauphase der Kuretenstraße', in R. Pillinger et al. (eds) *Efeso Paleocristiana e Bizantina – Frühchristliches und Byzantinisches Ephesos*, Rome, 104-20.

Thür, H., 2002a, 'Die Bauphasen der Wohneinheit 4 (und 6)', in F. Krinzinger (ed.) *Das Hanghaus 2 von Ephesos: Studien zu Baugeschichte und Chronologie*, Vienna, 41-66.

Thür, H., 2002b, 'Kontinuität und Diskontinuität im ephesischen Wohnbau der frühen Kaiserzeit', in C. Berns et al. (eds) *Patris und Imperium: kulturelle und politische Identität in den Städten der römischen Provinzen Kleinasiens in der frühen Kaiserzeit*, Leuven, 257-74.

Thür, H., 2005, 'Funktion der Räume in Bauphase IV', in H. Thür (ed.) *Hanghaus 2 in Ephesos: Die Wohneinheit 4*, Vienna, 415-26.

Tione, R., 1999, 'Le *domus* tardoantiche: nuovi elementi per l'interpretazione dell'edilizia abitativa attraverso la lettura stratigrafica degli elevati', *Mededelingen van het Nederlands Instituut te Rome: Antiquity* 58, 191-208.

Van Ossel, P., 1992, *Etablissements ruraux de l'Antiquité tardive dans le nord de la Gaule*, Paris.

Vanhaverbeke, H. and Waelkens, M. (eds), 2003, *The Chora of Sagalassos: The Evolution of the Settlement Pattern from Prehistoric until Recent Times*, Turnhout.

Vera, D., 1991, *Conductores domus nostrae, conductores privatorum.* Concentrazione fondiaria e redistribuzione della ricchezza nell'Africa tardoantica', *Institutions, société et vie politique dans l'empire romaine au IV siècle ap. J.C.*, Rome, 465-90.

Vera, D., 1994, 'Il sistema agrario tardoantico: un modello', in R. Francovich and G. Noyé (eds) *La Storia dell'Alto Medioevo italiano (VI-X secolo) alla luce dell'archeologia*, Florence, 136-8.

Vera, D., 1995, 'Dalla "villa perfecta" alla villa di Palladio: sulle trasformazioni del sistema agrario in Italia fra principato e dominato', *Athenaeum (Pavia)* 83, 189-211; 331-56.

Vera, D., 1997, 'Padroni, contadinni, contrati: *realia* del colonato tardoantico', in E. Lo Cascio (ed.) *Terre, propietari e contadini dell'impero romano*, Bari, 185-224.

Vera, D., 1999, 'I silenzi di Palladio e l'Italia: osservazioni sull'ultimo agronomo romano', *Antiquité tardive* 7, 283-97.

Bibliography

Vera, D., 2001, 'Sulla (ri)organizzazaione agraria dell'Italia meridionale in età imperiale', in E. Lo Cascio and D.S. Marino (eds) *Modalità insediative e strutture agrarie nell'Italia meridionale in età Romana, Atti del Convegno Internazionale,* Bari, 613-33.

Vogüé, M., 1865-77, *Syrie central: architecture civile et religieuse du Ier au VIIe siècle,* Paris.

Volpe, G., 2001, 'Linee di storia del paesaggio dell'Apulia romana: San Giusto e la valle del Celone', in E. Lo Cascio and D.S. Marino (eds) *Modalità insediative e strutture agrarie nell'Italia meridionale in età romana, Atti del Convegno Internazionale,* Bari, 315-61.

Volpe, G., 2002, 'Il mattone di *Iohannis* San Giusto (Lucera, Puglia)', in J.-M. Carrié and R. Lizzi Testa (eds) *'Humana Sapit': Études d'antiquité tardive offertes à Lellia Cracco Ruggini,* Turnhout, 79-93.

Volpe, G., 2005, 'A late Roman villa at Faragola, Italy', *Minerva* 17, 44-5.

Volpe, G., 2006, '*Stibadium* e *convivium* in una villa tardoantica (Faragola – Ascoli Satriano)', in M. Silvestrini, T.S. Vigorita and G. Volpe (eds) *Scritti in onore di Francesco Grelle,* Bari, 319-49.

Volpe, R., 2003, 'Via Labicana', in P. Pergola, R. Santangeli Valanzani and R. Volpe (eds) *Suburbium: il suburbio di Roma dalla crisi del sistema delle ville a Gregorio Magno,* Rome, 211-39.

Waelkens, M. et al., 2007, 'Two late antique residential complexes at Sagalossos', in L. Lavan, L. Özgenel and A. Sarantis (eds) *Housing in Late Antiquity: From Palaces to Shops,* Leiden, 495-513.

Wallace-Hadrill, A., 1994, *Houses and Society in Pompeii and Herculaneum,* Princeton.

Ward-Perkins, B., 1978, 'Luni – the decline and abandonment of a Roman town', in H.M.K. Blake, T.W. Potter and D.B. Whitehouse (eds) *Papers in Italian Archaeology I: The Lancaster Seminar,* Oxford, 313-21.

Ward-Perkins, B., 1998, 'The cities', in A. Cameron and P. Garnsey (eds) *Cambridge Ancient History,* vol. 13: *The Late Empire AD 337-425,* Cambridge, 371-410.

Ward-Perkins, J.B., 1954, 'Constantine and the origins of the Christian basilica', *Papers of the British School in Rome* 22, 69-90.

Ward-Perkins, J.B., 1974, *Roman Architecture,* New York.

Whittaker, C.R. and Garnsey, P., 1998, 'Rural life in the later Roman empire', in A. Cameron and P. Garnsey (eds) *Cambridge Ancient History,* vol. 13: *The Late Empire AD 337-425,* Cambridge, 277-311.

Whittow, M., 1990, 'Ruling the late Roman and early Byzantine city: a continuous history', *Past and Present* 129, 3-29.

Bibliography

Wickham, C., 2005, *Framing the Early Middle Ages: Europe and the Mediterranean 400-800*, Oxford.
Woolf, G., 1998, *Becoming Roman: The Origins of Provincial Civilization in Gaul*, Cambridge.
Yon, J.-B., 2002, *Notables de Palmyre*, Beirut.
Zaccaria Ruggiu, A., 1991, 'Abitazioni private e spazio pubblico. Il caso di Luni e di Conibriga', *Rivista di archeologia* 15, 97-110.

Index

Ammianus Marcellinus, 32
Antioch, 22
Apamea, 69; Maison du Cerf, 58
apartment building, 29, 72-3
Aphrodisias, 68-9, 73-4, 90;
Bishop's House, 44-6, 69
Apollonia, Palace of the Dux, 11-12, 28, 44-5
apse, 23, 31, 35, 55-60; as form, 60, 86, 95; bi-apsidal hall, 58; apsed hall, 26, 28-9, 45, 49-52, 54, 61, 64; *see also* reception room
Aquitaine, 30, 44, 77, 79, 90-2
architecture, medieval church, 21-2, 31, 85; Roman civic, 52, 55
Argos, Villa of the Falconer, 56
artifact analysis, 19-20, 38, 40, 42, 85
Asia Minor, 16, 43, 44
Athens, 37, 68-9, 73, 90; House of Proclus, 36; House between Dyonisiou Areopagitou and Makri Streets, 36; House between Irodou Attikou 2 and Basilissis Sofias Streets, 37
atrium, 46
audience hall, *see* apse: apsed hall; reception room

aula, see apse: apsed hall; reception room;
Ausonius, 78
axiality, 31, 49, 56-7; *see also* symmetry

Baldini Lippolis, Isabella, 29
Banaji, Jairus, 70, 81
baths, domestic, 17, 26, 51-4; public, 52, 54, 72
bedroom, 29, 47
Bianchi Bandinelli, Ranuccio, 16, 23
Bourdieu, Pierre, 85
Britain, 16, 30, 77, 79, 90-1, 93-4
Bulla Regia, 54, 72; House of the Hunt, 26-7, 44, 46; House of the New Hunt, 27, 50; House No. 3, 44
bureaucrats, imperial, 39, 65, 69-71, 76, 88-9, 91-5
Butrint, Triconch Palace, 11, 14-15, 35, 45

Caesarea Maritima, 68-9
Carrandini, Andrea, 25-6
Carranque, 13, 15, 30, 58
Carrié, Jean-Michele, 80
Carthage, 58, 72
ceremony, *see* ritual

Index

circulation patterns, 16-17, 20, 28-9, 32-3, 39, 42-54
cities, collapse of, 16, 28-9, 65, 68-9, 71-6; government, 28-32, 64-71; maintenance of, 17, 29, 68, 71-6
cliens, see clients
clients, 28, 62-4; *see also* patronage
colonate, late antique, 81
coloni, 25, 64, 78-82
competition between elites, 83, 87-9, 91, 95-8
Constantine, emperor, reforms of, 17, 66, 87-9, 90, 94, 96
Constantinople, 90, 93; imperial palace, 22
courtyard, 20, 31, 60, 95
cubiculum, see bedroom
Cuevas de Soria, 58-9
curator rei publicae, 70, 72, 94
curiales, 63, 65-70, 76, 91, 95

Danube, 30, 92
dining room, 20, 22, 28, 31-2, 39-46, 49, 51, 55-8, 62
Diocletian, emperor, reforms of, 17, 66, 88-9, 93-4
Djemila, 95; Maison aux Stucs, 99; Maison de Bacchus, 49, 53, 72; Maison d'Europe, 49, 53, 58, 72, 99; Maison de l'Ane, 98
dominus, 28, 30, 46, 63-4; relationships with *coloni*, 80-2
domus, urban, 17, 26-30, 37, 42, 64-76
Duval, Noël, 23
Dyggve, Enjar, 22

Ellis, Simon, 26-9, 42-6, 55-7, 61, 64-5, 77

emperor, 23, 30, 52
entrance, 31, 44, 46, 49, 54, 60, 77, 80
Ephesus, 68, 74-5, 90; Theatre House, 44, 47, 71, 74; House of the Governor, 58, 74; Hanghaus I, 38, 40, 71; Hanghaus II, 41-3, 48-9, 71
equestrian elites, 88-9
estates, management of, 26, 79-80, 82; imperial, 94; size, 77-9, 82
euergetism, see cities, maintenance of

Faragola, 94
fortifications, 92-3
functionalism, of rooms in house, 39-44, 86

Gárgoles, 58-9
Germany, 22
gold, 70-1
gsur, 17
Guidobaldi, Federico, 29

Hermopolis Register, 78
hierarchization, 16-17, 32-3, 39, 41, 46, 56-8, 61, 63-4, 77, 82-3, 86
Hispania, 30, 58, 77, 79, 90-2, 94
houses, Classical Greek, 11-12, 19-20, 32, 41; Roman Republican/imperial, 19, 32, 41, 46, 86, 95; Pompeian, 19-20, 47, 51

insula, see apartment building
Italy, 30, 77, 90-1, 93-4
iugum, 94

118

Index

Jones, A.H.M., 28, 65
Jurançon, 97

Kelly, Chris, 62
kitchen, 40
Krause, Jens-Uwe, 62

L'Orange, H.P., 22
Lamasba Tablets, 78
landholding, concentration of, 77-9
latrine, 40, 58
Lavin, Irving, 22
Lepelley, Claude, 66, 88
Lescar, 97
Libanius, 32, 61-5
Libya, 17
Ligures Baebiani Tablets, 78
Luni, 76

Magnesia Register, 78
Majorian, emperor, 57
Maximian, emperor, 23
Melania the Younger, 78
Mérida, 90; Morería, 38
Midi-Pyrénées, 95
Milan, 90
military elites, 88-9, 91, 95
military supply, 92-4
Montmaurin, 96
mosaics, 17, 23, 25-6, 31, 35, 58, 64, 80

Nérac, 44
North Africa, 22, 26, 42, 52, 54, 65-7, 76, 90, 93-4

Olynthos, 19-20
Ostia, 72-3, 90

painting, 17

palaces, imperial, 18, 20-6;
  palace, episcopal, 17
Palladius, 61
Pannonia, 77, 79, 90-4
pater tes poleos, 68, 74
patrocinium, see patronage
patronage, 16-7, 28, 43, 62-4
Paulinus of Nola, 60
periodization, 17, 31-2, 54, 60, 82, 85-7
peristyle, 17, 46, 50, 57, 58
Piazza Armerina, Villa di
  Casale, 11-13, 23-6, 30, 58, 64
politeuomenoi, see *curiales*
Pompeii, 19-20, 54; see also
  houses, Pompeian
Portus, 72-3
praefectus annonae, 73
praepositus pagi, 94
principales, 65-9, 71, 76
'private' space, 19, 28, 31-2, 39, 77, 86
proteuontes, see *principales*
provincial capitals, 69, 76, 90
provincial governors, 69-71, 76, 90
'public'/'private' dichotomy, 39, 46-51
Puglia, 93-4

reception room, 16-17, 28, 31-2, 35, 39-46, 49, 51-2, 58, 62, 80;
  see also apse: apsed hall
rents, 25, 30, 79
Rhineland frontier, 93
ritual, 61, 86; Christian, 22-3, 31; dining, 28, 32, 55-8;
  imperial, 22-3, 26, 29-30, 32
Rome, 29, 37, 55, 90, 93; House of the Valerii, 29-30; imperial palace (Flavian Palace), 29,

Index

51; San Paolo fuori le Mura, 25; suburban villas, 39
Rostovzteff, Michael, 16, 23, 88

Sagalassos, 41, 43
Salvian, 32, 62-3, 80
Sardis, 90
Saxon Shore Forts, 93
Sbeitla, Maison des Saisons, 58
sculpture, 17, 31
Seek, Otto, 65
senatorial elites, 63, 66-7, 87-9, 91, 96
Settefinestre, 25, 79
Settis, Salvatore, 26
Severan Marble Plan, 55
Sicily, 90, 91, 93
Sidonius Apollinaris, 32, 57-8
sigma courtyard, 95
slaves, villas and, 25, 79-80
Sofiana, 25
space syntax analysis, 20
Split, Palace of Diocletian, 21-2
stibadium, 28, 55-7
Stobi, House of Peristeria, 44
subdivision, of elite houses, 28, 49-50
Sulpicius Severus, 60
Swoboda, Karl, 22
Symmachus, 31
symmetry, 22-3, 57; *see also* axiality
Syria, 17, 21-2, 39, 68

tablinum, 46
taxes, 25, 80-2, 91, 93-4
tenants, *see coloni*
texts, and archaeology, 19-20, 31-2, 57-8, 61-2
Thébert, Yvon, 26-8, 46, 49-50, 52, 61, 77
Theodosian Code, 62, 66, 80-1
Thugga, 54
Timgad, 70
transept, 26
triclinium, *see* dining room
triconch, 22, 35, 45
Trier, 90
Tunisia, 49

Vandals, 93
Veleia Tablets, 78
Vera, Domenico, 79
Villa Fortunatus, 44
villas, rural, 17, 30-1, 43, 59, 62, 64, 77-82, 90-5
Vitruvius, 19
Volcei Register, 78
Volubilis, Maison aux demi-Colonnes, 49, 51; Maison à l'Ouest du Palais du Governeur, 49-50

wealth, and houses, 38-9

Xanthos, Northeast House, 41
Xenophon, 19

www.ingramcontent.com/pod-product-compliance
Lightning Source LLC
Chambersburg PA
CBHW051815230426
43672CB00012B/2739